THE LORD JESUS CHRIST
KING OF KINGS AND
THE LORD OF LORDS

I hereby totally surrender all that I have and am, or shall ever have or be, completely to Jesus Christ (all other conditions and terms of this contract to be filled in later by the Lord Jesus Christ).

-
-
-
-
-
-
-
-
-
-
-
-
-
-

Date _____

Witness _____**GOD**_____

Signature _ _ _ _ _ _ _ _ _

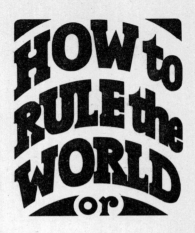

"Seek First the Kingdom of God" ~ Jesus

"Thy kingdom come, Thy will be done,
in this earth—as in heaven."

The Lord In You—NOW!!!

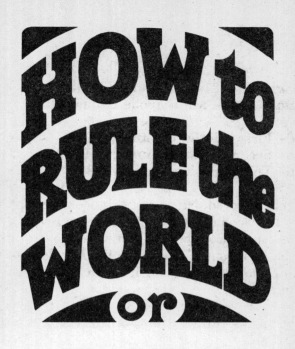

HOW to RULE the WORLD (or)

"Seek 1st the
Kingdom
of God"~Jesus

by John Roy Bohlen

ACKNOWLEDGMENTS

Special thanks to Marty Solarz and Jeannine Potter for much dedicated typing; to the many dear ones who have helped birth this book in their travail, to our parents and grandparents who led such godly lives. To the Apostles and Prophets and people of God who have loved me. To Ed and Sonnie Hussman for giving and encouraging. To great ones like Louis L'Amour, Len Ravenhill, Dr. Bob Smith, Bethel College and Bethany Fellowship. To my children Joey, Kari, Dawn Joy, and Josh who love me unconditionally. To David and Joan Turnidge and boys. David made his entire programming and computer sales company (Programming Service Associates) available and dedicated countless hours at his word processors, typing, making corrections and suggestions. To Rolf and Kent Garborg of Successful Living for their support and encouragement, to David Dirkes and family for undergirding, to all everywhere who have given even a cup of cold water in the name of a disciple. To Evangelist Bob Hart, (we saved each other from drowning), to Wells and Sandy Wright and boys for being our friend, to Cookie and John McGinnity, Bill and Carmella Fogerty, and the Carpenter Clan, and especially more than any other human beings—deep thanks to my wonderful wife Karen who cheered for me before I made touchdowns and who cheers for me now before the game is over. And most of all, Thank You, Mighty Right Now God, Creator and King of all the Universe—Lord Jesus Christ, for everything!!!

DEDICATION

To God

and

1. To: Those of you my friends who will pay the price to rule and reign on the throne forever with Christ the Creator King of all the Universe. I salute you as my brothers and sisters.

2. To: You dear ones who will continue to be indifferent, passive, unresponsive and lukewarm to the King's command. Unless you change completely and quickly, Christ Jesus our Gentle Saviour Shepherd King promises to spit you out of His mouth. Revelation 3:16

3. To: God's enemies and mine who are involved in your own personal or religious or financial or political kingdom all of which will be taken completely over or destroyed by the Creator King of All the Universe. I invite you to switch to the winning team while you can, 'cauz forever is a long, long time to burn. God commands all men everywhere to repent. Revelation chapter 11.

To each one of you—this book is lovingly dedicated. See you at the judgment seat of Christ.

EXPLANATION

—Unless otherwise noted: all scriptures are quoted from the New American Standard Bible. © The Lockman Foundation — 1960, 1962, 1963, 1971, 1972, 1973, 1975, are used by permission.

—Brackets ([ ]) in the scriptural quotations indicate the use of author's own words.

—All quotations from the King James Version are identified as (KJ).

—All author's paraphrases or adaptations are identified as (JB).

—All quotations from the Amplified New Testament are identified as (AMP), and are also used by permission from the Lockman Foundation, © 1958.

—Each chapter's scriptural references, and other footnotes, if any, are indicated at the conclusion of each chapter.

A quotation is taken from the book **To The Far Blue Mountains**, by Louis L'Amour. Chapter 30. Copyright © 1976 by Louis L'Amour. Used by permission of Bantam Books, Inc. All rights reserved.

Also, a quotation is taken from Leonard Ravenhill's book, **Why Revival Tarries**, published by Bethany Fellowship, Inc., 6820 Auto Club Road, Mpls., Mn 55438, and is used by permission.

We recommend all of the books by the above authors.

You will find the Questionnaire and the Review Questions interesting. They may be used at your discretion, for personal study and learning, or in any group training situation. We recommend that you at least read them.

We also are respectfully open to any suggestions or questions that may improve this presentation. Enjoy the meat, set aside the bones. We don't know all there is to know about God yet. Our address is found on the back cover. The Lord will be with you as you read.

Please enjoy this book—then rise in the strength of the Lord and go forth to do mighty exploits for thy God!!!

ILLUSTRATIONS BY
CHRIS WOLD DYRUD

1. (Cover) "HOW TO RULE THE WORLD" or "SEEK 1st THE KINGDOM OF GOD"
2. (Contract) "KINGDOM CONTRACT" or "HAVE YOU SIGNED THE CONTRACT?!."
3. (Door) "WHO'S THAT KNOCKING AT YOUR DOOR?!."
4. (Cross) "WERE YOU THERE WHEN THEY CRUCIFIED MY LORD?!."
5. (Elephant) "WHO WAS THE FLEA'S FRIEND?!."
6. (Hawg) "DO YOU LIKE 'HAWG WALLERS' ?!."
7. (Gun) "EVER SEEN A CANNIBAL?!."
8. (Movies) "THE DEVIL WITH THE MOVIES?!."
9. (Cartoons) "DID THE DEVIL MAKE YOU DO IT?!."
   —Honey & Toast
   —Abbot Smacks Costello
   —Even to the Thickness of a Cobweb
   —What you see ain't what you get
   —Hitchhikers can be bad
10. (For Sale) "IF A MAN HAS A SELLOUT PRICE, SATAN WILL COME UP WITH THE SILVER."

THE KINGDOM OF GOD
TABLE OF CONTENTS

Hint, Hunch or Humbug
Abbot & Costello * * Laurel & Hardy

ABOUT THE AUTHOR

John Roy Bohlen grew up on a primitive Iowa farm with virgin timber, Indian Mounds, hard work and a love for God. Both blessed and handicapped by a deep hunger for God, he early learned and chose to build his life on two things: The total believeability of the Bible as the Word of God, and the total **Lordship of Jesus Christ** in everything. He tells about an incredible meeting with the Lord during his senior year at Bethel College in 1960 in St. Paul, from which he graduated with a degree in philosophy under Dr. Bob Smith and a minor in psychology. He met Karen at Bethany Fellowship Missionary Training Center in Bloomington, Mn., from which they graduated in 1964. Karen is a Registered X-ray Technician, and gives training on the women's ministry to their husbands and children.

God has used men like Len Ravenhill, Jack Winter, Dr. Bob Smith as well as many apostles and prophets, intercessors and enemies as an encouragement. John was a probation officer for L.A. county for 6 years, and has known various phases of construction and real estate. He has helped establish a number of churches, and pioneered and pastored a metropolitan church in Phoenix. Two 40-day fasts and much seeking of God resulted in the establishing of ministries focusing on the Great Commission and Matt. 6:33. John read the entire Bible through more than four times during the writing of this book.

He and Karen are blessed with four children: Joseph, Kari, Dawn Joy, and Joshua. The family travels extensively, (they moved 24 times in the first 12 years of marriage), and they minister the Word, sing as a family, conduct seminars with others of a similar Kingdom vision, on the Lordship of Christ, Marriage and the Family, Discipleship Training, Worship and Evangelism. These seminars are available in your area.

This book is not religious, but spiritual; is not a sedative, but is intense; at times cutting like a razor or hitting like a sledge-hammer. Another book is forthcoming on Marriage and the Family.

May you have an Abundant entrance into THE KINGDOM OF GOD!!!!

PREFACE

Just for fun, project your thoughts ahead in time to that day soon coming when you will stand before the Great & Mighty Judge of all the Universe. We all will have Him to face you know. How will it be for you? How will it go? The Bible has so much to say about that day. This book will help you prepare for that final exam, and will help you pass the final test—the consuming fire of God!

The Bible says, "Every person's work will be tried by fire, of what sort it is: wood, hay, stubble, gold, silver, precious stones."* But like our school exams, we must prepare now for that future test.

The rewards and penalties are great! The lessons shared in this book can make all the difference! If these principles are followed, you are guaranteed an abundant entrance into the Kingdom of God; and will be chosen by God to RULE THE WORLD! ! !

*I Cor. 3:12-15 (JB)

KINGDOM OF GOD DISCIPLESHIP TRAINING

* * * (Please try to do this rejoicingly) * * *

1. Have you ever given your life completely to the Lord Jesus Christ?
2. Are you willing to give yourself to Him now, 100%?
3. What is a "disciple" of the Lord Jesus? Are You one? Give yourself a grade.
4. If Jesus walked up to you like He did to Matthew and said, "follow Me", would you?
5. Are you willing to do *anything* God would tell you to do?
6. What is the longest you have fasted only on water?
7. Have you ever stayed up all night to pray? About how many times?
8. How is a person "Born Again"? (tell how to be saved.)
9. Have you been born again? Are you now right with God?
10. How long have you been born again?
11. Who was influential or involved in your new birth? How did it happen?

12. Approximately how many people have you personally led to Christ in your lifetime of ministry? Please try to estimate.

13. Have you ever been filled with the Holy Spirit? If so, how recently? When first?

14. Are you full of God right now? Grade yourself with a percentage, 1-100%

15. About how many people have you tried to present the plan of salvation to: a) In your life? b) In the last year? c) 6 months? d) Month? e) Week?

16. Can a person lose their salvation? Please explain?

17. What do you think hell is like?

18. Have you ever wept for the lost? When was the last time? Are you burdened for them?

19. Have you ever read the Bible all the way through? Every verse?

20. How many times?

21. How recently?

22. What is the "Great Commission"?

23. To whom does the Great Commission apply?

24. How much are you willing to give up to see the Great commission fulfilled?

25. List as many ways as possible to do the Great Commission. We are always looking for ideas.

26. What is the "gospel"? Is it the same as the gospel of the Kingdom?

27. What, in just a few words, is the Kingdom of God?

28. What does it mean, "Seek first the Kingdom of God"?
29. How will the Kingdom of God be established?
30. When?
31. Through whom?
32. Where?
33. Christ promises 100 fold return on what we give to the Kingdom of God. In terms of banking percentages, what percent return would this be on your investment? Interested?
34. Do you think it is possible to live without sinning?
35. Do you have any resentment or unforgiveness towards anyone?
36. Are you aware of any unconfessed or unforgiven sin in your life?
37. Do you have any problems too deep or personal to tell anyone? What are they?
38. Would you like or do you need personal counseling or ministry about anything?
39. What are the most important things to you in your life? Please list at least 7 to 12 things in order of importance.
40. Please list what you think Christ took of ours with Him to the cross?
41. If something is God's will . . . will it happen?
42. What are your ministries, or gifts in the Lord?

43. What ministries, ambitions or gifts would you like to have?

44. Would you like to have a seminar in your area on discipleship training, or the material in this book?

45. Do you have any suggestions for this questionnaire? This book?

INTRODUCTION

KINGDOM OF GOD

A prophet friend of mine, who is kinda ugly and has a lot to learn, but who has also learned a lot, says, "Well now, a book on the Kingdom of God? I'd say that's takin' in quite a swath by any man's standards, but then again, sometimes a feller kin do some things through Christ who strengthens him." Well, sir (or ma'am as the case may be), that there is jes' what this here feller is aimin' to do . . . **something** through Christ who strengthens him. You see, some folks have a god that is tooooooo small, who is only able to supply some of their needs. Their bible is shot so full o' holes that it's 'holey'. Then there's others that are downright idol worshippers. Yup, their idol is their problem, greater than their little god's ability to solve it. Or also, maybe the idol is named 'Own Self' or 'My Inability' or 'Sinful Nature', all of them greater than their little god.

But this here feller's got a GOD that's greater than His worshipper's weaknesses or inability or sin. Those idol worshippers now, their bible says, "I can do some things through my little god", or "Some things are possible with little god", or "My little god just might supply some of my need (from his almost busted bank account)", or "In some of these here things I'm almost a conqueror", or "Try to be perfect". (All of these here quotes is from the Reversed Stupid Version of the Unbeliever's Bible.)

To quote my friend, Leonard Ravenhill, from his book, *Why Revival Tarries,* "One of these days, some simple soul will pick up the Word of God, read it, believe it, and then the rest of us will be embarrassed." Dear one, the Lord Jesus Christ is promised a perfect Bride, the Lord Jesus is worthy of a perfect Bride, and, praise God, He's going to have a perfect Bride!!! Hallelujahweh!!!*

The eyes of the Lord God are looking to and fro through all the earth for those who will just BELIEVE Him. Simply believe and obey Him. That's the Kingdom of God—simply doing and being what God wants. Amen.

---

*Please don't be offended at the author's occasional use of this or "ALLELUJAHVAH". Just bear with him, it's a personal coinage used for his own benefit, and perhaps the Lord's. It means, "I worship You, my Mighty Right Now God!"

1

GOD'S PRIORITIES
or
FIRST THINGS FIRST
or
"SEEK YE FIRST THE KINGDOM OF GOD!!!"

"Seek ye first the kingdom of God", He says. And when He says it, His voice is as the sound of many waters, as the sound like the Niagara Falls up close. "Seek ye first the kingdom of God and His [right-ness]" (a), He says to us. I said, "Lord, what about food, clothing and shelter?" Jesus said, "Seek ye first the kingdom of God and His righteousness and all these things shall be added unto you" (a)

Then God's voice again sounds like the Niagara Falls from the mouth of the Wind Tunnels on the Canadian side directly underneath the falls, "Go ye into all the world, make disciples of all nations, teaching them to obey every thing that I have commanded you." (b) I said,

"O.K., but . . ." Again the still small voice seems to roar so quietly that it is deafening! "**All authority has been given to Me in heaven and on earth! Go therefore and make disciples of all the nations, baptizing them in the name of the Father and the Son and the Holy Spirit, teaching them to observe all that I commanded you: and lo, I am with you always, even to the end of the age**" (b)

I had completed my second 40 day fast on just water. I decided to believe the Bible, but had been frustrated that so many of the promises weren't nitty gritty experiential gut-level reality. I had turned 40 and got a real bad case of "mid-life-crisis". My pal, Joey, came to me later and asked me, "Dad, what's a male mental pause?" I said, "That's like when a guy starts becoming forgetful."

But when I turned 40, all of a sudden I became terrified! Where had all those green years gone? To quote my friend, Louis L'Amour, "Where go the years? Down what tunnel of time are poured the precious days? We are young and the fires within us burn bright. All the world lies before us and nothing is too great to be done, no challenge too awesome. Then, suddenly the days are no more and the time that remains is little indeed." (From chapter 30 of *To The Far Blue Mountains*.) Why, it seemed that only yesterday morning I had graduated from Bethel College ('61), yesterday noon we got married, finished Bethany Fellowship, and lived happily ever after

('64), yesterday afternoon Joseph was born ('66),
seconds later Kari came ('68), then Dawn Joy
('70), and Joshua ('72). But now, today noon, I'm
40 already. I said, shaking my head from side to
side like some delirious dumb brute animal,
"Where has all the time gone?" Yesterday morning I was a kid on the Iowa farm dreaming of the
miracles I'd work; only yesterday when the men
of God told me of the places I'd minister, only
last evening when the English teacher at Bible
School asked us to write a theme on what we intended to be doing in five or ten years. She scold-
ed me for not being realistic when I had sincerely
written how that by the age of 31 I expected to be
healing the sick, raising the dead, traveling in the
Holy Spirit, ministering supernaturally in the
languages of the people by the Holy Spirit, seeing
tens of thousands of people being born again.
That was 20 years ago. Now I was 40 and scared
stiff! I thought, "I haven't committed the act of
adultery, nor have I ever been drunk—yet my sin
is very great." I remembered where James said,
"To him that knoweth to do good and doeth it
not, to him it is sin" (c) Brother, I'd known a
whole lot of good to do, but had not done it. I
thought of the Apostle Paul saying, "I've been
faithful to the heavenly vision . . . I've fought the
good fight, I've finished the course, henceforth is
laid up for me a crown of righteousness that no
man can take . . . The blood of no man is on my
hands." (d) I couldn't say that. I've known to do

a whole lot of good and done it not. Young buck—yesterday I was reckless, handsome, (I really was), and strong, filled with dreams and visions of what we were going to do for God. Now I was bald-headed and pot-bellied and 'hain't really did much for Jesus.' It scared me so bad I went on this 40 day fast—no food or juice or pills—just distilled water. (I had gone on another one in 1972 while working as a probation officer for L. A. County.) I wanted to minimize these serious sins of lassitude, insipidity and indecision.

One major thing happened because of this 40 day fast (besides losing weight): I decided to do the will of God. I mean **really** decided. I don't know if it affected me mentally or emotionally or what, but I **decided** to do the will of God. I mean **really decided!** Oh, I had decided before, many times. I remember going to an apostle one time and saying, "Do you witness that I should now begin walking in the words that God has spoken and confirmed over my life?" He said, "I was wondering when you were going to start." But I just hadn't meant that much business. Oh, I had gone to church, sometimes ten times a week; prayed, often before the sun came up and sometimes through the night; and I had ministered some, three or four brief missionary trips to Mexico, several years as a pastor, also preaching here and there, etc. But there was just too much good I knew to do but had not done—too much of that serious kind of sinning that wouldn't look so good tomorrow noon at the judgment seat of Christ. "Son," I could imagine the Lord saying, "Why did you not **do** the blueprint I had for you? Why did you not **do** the living Works or the creative words I gave you to **do** and speak?"

There is a Greek word for sin—"hamartano" which means "to miss the mark" or the bull's-eye. How sad to miss the mark or the plan or blueprint God planned for us during our days, months and years! The Bible says God has living words and Works planned for us. Jesus said in John 5:19, 30 and other places that He always only did what He saw the Father doing and spoke only what He heard the Father speaking. I decided that this way of life was for me also, and determined that from now on—no matter what or who—**I would do God's will as best as I could determine it. God have mercy on my soul!!!!**

I remembered that it's possible to be so good that you are good for nothing. I thought of the 'one-talent-man' who had the talent, the commission, but brought the same talent back to God unmultiplied. I believe he was a pretty average Christian. You remember what happened to him? He got set adrift in, and exiled to, the blackness of outer space with wailing and gnashing of teeth—forever! Can you imagine what that would be like?

So, out of 40 years of walking with God, two complete 40 day fasts, (e) over 20 years being full of the Holy Spirit (theoretically), I made two decisions. They both border on insanity, I guess. A disciple, Jeff, asked me one day, "John, how do you **know** the will of God?" I said, "Be insanely committed to **do** the will of God. (I believe the **real** insanity is **not** doing the will of God.) A guy called me 'weird' one time, at which I responded, "Friend, if the rest of the world is 'normal,' you just paid me a compliment! Anyway, I **decided** to **do** two things with the rest of my life:

1. Matt. 6:33—Seek first the Kingdom of God and His righteousness. (JB)
2. Matt. 28:19-20—Go into all the world, make disciples of all nations, teaching them to observe all He commands us. (JB)

Well then, I thought, "If I'm going to spend the rest of my life seeking first the Kingdom of God, I'd better find out what this Kingdom of God is. Oh, I had some vague ideas, but I had to **know** . . . really know. I mean, I will not base my whole life on some vague idea. So I got out my big four inch thick concordance and looked up every verse on the Kingdom of God, Kingdom of Heaven, the King, Kingdoms, Kings, Lord (over 7000 verses on Yahweh or Yahvah alone), Lordship of Christ, etc. I did the same thing with all the verses on disciple, disciples, discipleship, etc., because I thought, "If I'm going to go into all the world and make disciples of all nations, I should know what a 'disciple' is." During this time, I read the entire Bible through 4 times. (e) Many months I studied, and I came to the following conclusions:

1. **THE KINGDOM OF GOD IS THE MOST IMPORTANT THING IN THE BIBLE.**
2. **IT MUST BE TAUGHT IN ALL THE WORLD BEFORE THE END CAN COME.**
3. **HARDLY ANYBODY, INCLUDING CHRISTIANS, KNOWS WHAT THE KINGDOM OF GOD IS.**

Please pray with me.

Heavenly Father, tomorrow noon, when I stand before the Mighty and Awesome Judge of all the Universe, I want to pass the test and have Christ say, "Well done." Grant that I qualify now for an abundant entrance into His Kingdom then. In Jesus' name, Amen.

---

a) Matt. 6:33
b) Matt. 28:18-20; Mark 16:15-18
c) James 4:17 (KJ)
d) Acts 20:25-26; 26:19; II Tim. 4:5-8 (JB)
e) My mention here of fasting and reading the Word are not deliberate intentions to brag. I am willing to lose the reward for doing these—if by example and teaching I can be a blessing to you.

Review Questions

HOW IMPORTANT?!

1. Make a list of the 12 most important things in your life in order of importance.
2. What does Matt. 6:33 say?
3. What is the Kingdom of God? (Be brief)
4. What are some of the things that will be added unto us if we seek first God's Kingdom?
5. Where has the Kingdom of God been on your priority list?
6. From now on, where will the Kingdom of God be on your priority list?
7. Name a kind of sin other than a sin where you do something wrong.
8. What is the Greek word for sin which means missing the mark or bull's-eye?
9. What is meant by "Living Works"?
10. What is meant by "Dead Works"?
11. What happens if we speak "idle words"?
12. What is meant by "idle words"?
13. What was the "modus operandi" or method by which Christ Jesus did the Father's will?
14. What should ours be?
15. Did the "one talent man" have a relationship with the Lord?
16. Name three elements of that relationship.
17. What two things happened to him when he didn't produce?
18. Describe what you think it would be like to

be exiled and set adrift in the blackness of outer space.

19. What is the Great Commission?
20. Where is it found?
21. Do you think that the Great Commission applies to you?
22. Please give a definition of a "disciple" of the Lord Jesus.
23. Who did Jesus say His brothers, mother and sisters are?
24. Who did Jesus say His "friends" are?
25. Who did Jesus say could not be His disciple?
26. Are you a disciple of the Lord Jesus Christ?
27. Give yourself a grade in percentages—1 to 100%?
28. Jesus said that all people would be able to tell if we are His disciples by what?
29. Jesus said that we would do what as proof of our love for Him?
30. Complete this verse, "Herein is My Father glorified, that _____ _____ _____ _____ and so prove to be My disciples.

2

MOST IMPORTANT IS THE "KINGDOM OF GOD"!

Most important is the Kingdom of God! Jesus said, "Seek ye **first** the Kingdom of God and His righteousness" and [everything will be all right!!!] Matt. 6:33 (KJ). In the Lord's Prayer, we pray, "Thy Kingdom come . . . [on] earth as it is in Heaven" Matt. 6:9 (KJ). Jesus taught more about the Kingdom of God than anything else. So did John the Baptist, John, Mark, Luke, and Matthew, the twelve, the seventy, Daniel, the early disciples, and the last day disciples! There are literally thousands and Thousands and **thousands** of scripture verses relating to the Kingdom of God and the Lordship of Christ! The word 'Lord' or **Yahweh** or **Yahvah**, meaning the Mighty Right Now God, is used more than 7000 times alone!!!

And yet, almost **no** Christians know what the Kingdom of God is! Talk about a need in the marketplace!!! Someone said, "To be a success, find a need in the marketplace and fill it!" I have asked many book sellers, handlers and distributors if they knew of any books on the Kingdom of God and they have said, "No." (Although I know of two or three good ones.) One book I am aware of reads like a doctoral thesis for seminary graduates. In our seminars and ministry we have asked·the question, "What is the Kingdom of God?" Almost no one seems to know! We also have seen books with the title, "The Kingdom of God," but they end up mostly talking about something else! In other words, we deeply feel the need for more teaching in the church and through the church to the regions beyond on God's priorities, the Great Commission, and the Kingdom of God!!!

Let's look at only a few scriptures that speak to the importance of the Kingdom of God: "The *Lord is King forever* and ever . . ."—Ps. 10:16. "For God is the *King of all the earth* . . ."—Ps. 47:7. ". . . my eyes have seen *the King,* [**Yahvah Sabbaoth**]—the Lord of Hosts [or Armies]."— Isa. 6:5. "Who would not fear thee, *O King* of the nations."—Jer. 10:7. "The Lord is the true God; He is the living God and *the Everlasting King*: at His wrath the earth quakes, and the nations cannot endure His indignation"—Jer. 10:10. "And the Lord shall be *King over all* the earth . . . And it shall come to pass that every one that is left of all the nations . . . shall even go up from year to year to worship *the King,* the

Lord of hosts [armies], and to keep the feast of tabernacles"—Zech. 14:9, 16 (KJ). "Repent, for the *Kingdom of Heaven* is at hand" (John the Baptist) Matt. 3:2. Jesus said, "Repent, for the *Kingdom of Heaven* is at hand . . . And Jesus was going about in all Galilee, teaching in their synagogues, and proclaiming the *Gospel of the Kingdom*, and healing every kind of disease and every kind of sickness among the people"—Matt. 4:17b, 23. ". . .He went throughout every city and village, preaching and shewing the glad tidings of the *Kingdom of God:* and the twelve were with Him"—Luke 8:1 (KJ). "And the people . . . followed Him: and He received them, and spake unto them of the *Kingdom of God*, and healed them that had need of healing"—Luke 9:11 (KJ). "This *Gospel of the Kingdom* shall be preached in the *whole world* for a witness to all the nations, and *then* the end shall come" Matt. 24:14.

Look at this verse again: "And this Good News of the Kingdom will be preached throughout the whole world as a testimony to all the nations, and then will come the end" Matt. 24:14 (AMP). Is it possible that if this good news of the Kingdom of God is not preached in all the world for a witness, that the end will not come? If being born again is only a part of it—only the beginning—and if the good news of the Kingdom of God is so important, we'd best find out what it is.

But let's look at this thing of priorities. What is the most important thing? Jesus said to seek first the Kingdom of God! Tell me, if you were to make a list of the things that are important to you in your life, where would the Kingdom of God be on your priority list?

The Bible says there is a day soon coming when we will all stand before the Righteous Judge of all the universe to be judged by only one thing: "Did we do the will of God? Did we seek first the Kingdom of God? To what extent did our lives conform to God's plan and blueprint?" Because *all* of us will be judged by what was important to us: by our priorities, by what we did with our money, time, talents, potential, energies, possessions and life. God will say, "How much of My plan and will did you fulfill?"

Thus saith the Lord, "There will be no excuse for not doing the plan and will of God."

So, I ask, "Where is the will, plan, and Kingdom of God on your priority list (or things important in your life)?" God says it must be first!

But for many years, the Kingdom of God was number four on my priority list. Food, clothing and shelter for my family came first, second and third. I said, "I will provide for my family first, and will serve God with the time, money and energy left over." But at age 40, I suddenly realized that over half of my expected years were gone and that there hadn't been enough time, money or energy left over to fulfill the great plan and commission for my life!!!

No excuse will stand before the judgment seat

of Christ, but the one excuse I believe most people will try to give for not having done the will of God, the plan and blueprint of God, the living words and Works of God, or for not having sought first the Kingdom of God, is that they were too busy providing food, clothing and shelter for their family. But Jesus said that He would take care of these things if we "Seek first the Kingdom of God and His righteousness" (Matt. 6:33). II Timothy 2:4 says, "No soldier in active service entangles himself in the affairs of every day life, so that he may please the one who enlisted him."

Jesus said that it is not possible to serve both God *and* money (Matt. 6:24, Luke 16:13). Matthew 6:33 is preceded by a thorough discussion of food, clothing and shelter. But Jesus said that He would take care of these things if we obeyed Him and put God's will and Kingdom first. How sad, to think we spent a lifetime seeking and doing a lesser thing that would have been added to us anyway, had we only done the will of God: Seeking *First* His Kingdom.

Take the parable of the man who sold "all that he had" to buy a field with a treasure in it (Matt. 13:44). With the treasure now his, he can buy far more than a hundred times more than he had before!

So we see that the Kingdom of God is the most important thing to God! How important is the Kingdom of God to you???

Statistics show that the Christian church is

further behind than she's ever been. I mean, there is a greater percentage of unsaved people unreached with the Gospel of the Kingdom in the earth today than at any time since the first century! There may be a few more Christians, but the heathen population has increased far faster than the "Born Again" population.

Jesus said that up until now, the Kingdom of God suffers violence, but violent people take it by force! (Matt. 11:12) In other words, The Kingdom of God and the will of God has not been established and accomplished, and won't be, until we become intense enough and mean business enough to seek first His Kingdom!!!

Three of our four children are old enough to baby-sit now, and we are concerned that they act responsibly. Suppose the parents leave instructions for the dishes to be done after the children are in bed. Then the home catches fire and the baby-sitter says, "Even though the kids are being burned, I need to do the dishes." You say, "That's silly!" But it is no more silly than the activities of our life out of the first will of God, while the world burns. Bill Bright has said that we are like picture straighteners in a burning building.

But one of these days, people are going to become intense enough about the wrong that the Kingdom of God is suffering and we will rise up in the fiery white hot zeal of the Lord of the armies (hosts) to right the wrong and take the

Kingdom for the Lord, fulfill God's Great Commission, and seek first the Kingdom of God!!!

God's Kingdom is number 1 on His list of priorities—where is it on yours???

Lord Jesus, show me the importance of the Kingdom of God. Thank You, Lord. Amen.

A friend of mine said to a friend of his, "You've got your priorities screwed up."

Review Questions

MOST IMPORTANT IS THE KINGDOM OF GOD!

1. Where is the Kingdom of God in your priority list?
2. What was the main theme of Christ and the disciples and the Apostle Paul in their teaching?
3. What is the Name of God given over 7000 times in the Old Testament?
4. Have you ever read any good books on the Kingdom of God? What are their titles?
5. Do you remember hearing any teachings or sermons on the Kingdom of God?
6. Did you know what the Kingdom of God was before now?
7. What is the "Gospel of the Kingdom"?
8. Is the "Gospel of the Kingdom" different from the "Gospel" as you have known it?
9. Will the end come if this Gospel of the Kingdom is not preached in all the world for a witness to all the nations?
10. Whose responsibility is it to preach this Gospel of the Kingdom in all the world?
11. How soon could this be accomplished?
12. What sort of sacrifices could you specifically make to see this goal accomplished?

13. Will you?
14. Does the Great Commission apply to you? Why? How? When?
15. Who will be judged at the judgment day?
16. What will you/they be judged for?
17. What will probably be the main excuse given by Christians for not having done the will of God? What's yours? Will these excuses stand?
18. A man told me that last year he was only doing about 10% of the will of God and the rest was compromise. Now he says his life is only about 60 to 40% compromise with what he thinks he should be doing. Question: What % of God's will, plan and blueprint for your life would you say you are doing? (The remaining % would be compromise.)
19. What do you think the verse means, "You cannot serve God and mammon"? (Luke 16:13; Matt. 6:24)
20. What does II Tim. 2:4 mean?
21. Do you think the person was able to recap or regain more than his original investment in Matt. 13:44?
22. What do you think the main reason is that the Great Commission has not been fulfilled?
23. What is meant by the word "violence" both times it is used in Matt. 11:12?
24. What is meant by the statement that we have been like picture straighteners in a burning building?

3

WHAT AND WHEN AND WHERE IS THE KINGDOM OF GOD?

After years of prayer, reading, study, revelation, and experience, we have concluded that **the Kingdom of God is what God is the King of**. The Kingdom of God is whatever God is the King over. The Kingdom of God is, the Lordship of Christ is, whatever God or Christ is the boss over.

In other words, if a person invites Christ and God to be the Lord, Chief, Boss, Saviour, Master, Commander, King over his or her life, and lives according to the King's desires, and does what the King wants, then to that extent, that life will be an expression of the Kingdom of God on the earth today.

To the extent that a person (or family) makes God the King over their family, and King over what that wife, husband and children say and do by saying, "God is the King over this family. We shall function under His Lordship, living by His rules and His love, and relate to one another as

King Jesus wishes," then to that extent—that family becomes a literal, visible expression of the Kingdom of God! If a person says and does the same thing with his property, possessions, and business, insisting that it be run **exactly** by the leading of the Holy Spirit (this, of course, necessitates knowing God's voice), then that person's property, possessions, and business becomes a literal, visible demonstration of the Kingdom of God in the right now!

This same principle applies to a church body. Many churches do not conform to the King's pattern or blueprint for the church as given in the New Testament. Thus there comes a choice for those involved in such a church. They can either experience voluntary change (in some cases the word would be "upheaval" or renovation). As with all the Kingdoms of this world—the religious Kingdoms—must also come under the awesome Lordship of Christ the King—as to pattern and practice—or be destroyed. If a church decides, **really** decides to do according to the will of God and the Word of God and the teaching of the Spirit of God, no matter what; worshiping as Christ wants; working, warring as God wants; giving as God wants; being organized as Christ wants; insisting that the ministries and members function and relate to each other and love each other as He wants; then to that same degree and extent that God is King of that congregation, that church will be a living demonstration, in the right now, of the Kingdom of God. Christ said, "But if I, with the finger of God cast out devils, no doubt the Kingdom of God is come upon you" Luke 11:20 (KJ). And in another place, "The Kingdom of God is within you." Lk. 17:21 (ANT)

KINGDOM OF GOD

Selected verses from the New Testament

"But seek ye first the *Kingdom of God*, and His righteousness; and all these things shall be added unto you" Matt. 6:33 (KJ).

"Or do you not know that the unrighteous shall *NOT inherit the Kingdom of God?* Do not be deceived: neither fornicators, nor idolators, nor adulterers, nor effeminate, nor homosexuals, nor thieves, nor covetous, nor drunkards, nor revilers, nor swindlers, shall inherit the *Kingdom of God*" I Cor. 6:9, 10.

"Now the works of the flesh are manifest, which are these: adultery, fornication, uncleanness, lasciviousness, idolatry, witchcraft, *hatred, variance, emulations, wrath, strife*, seditions, heresies, *envyings*, murders, drunkenness, *revellings*, and such like: of the which I tell you before, as I have also told you in time past, that they which do such things shall *not* inherit the *Kingdom of God*" Gal. 5:19-21 (KJ).

"So that you may walk in a manner worthy of the God who calls you into His own *Kingdom* and glory. And for this reason we also constantly thank God that when you received from us the word of God's message, you accepted it not as the word of men, but for what it really is, the Word of God, which also performs its work in you [mightily] who believe" I Th. 2:12, 13.

"Now unto the King *eternal*, immortal, invisible, the only wise God, be honour and glory for ever and ever. Amen" I Tim. 1:17 (KJ).

"And he who overcomes, and he who keeps My deeds until the end, to him I will give *authority over the nations*; and *he shall rule them with a rod of iron*, as the vessels of the potter are broken to pieces, as I also have received authority from My Father" Rev. 2:26, 27.

"The kingdoms of this world are become the Kingdoms of our Lord, and of His Christ; and He shall reign for ever and ever" Rev. 11:15 (KJ).

"And she gave birth to a son, a *male child*, who is *to rule all the nations* with a rod of iron. . ." Rev. 12:5.

". . . great and marvelous are Thy works, O Lord God, the Almighty; righteous and true are Thy ways *Thou King of the nations*. Who will not fear, O Lord, and glorify Thy name? For Thou alone art holy; for all the nations will come and worship before Thee, for Thy righteous acts have been revealed" Rev. 15:3, 4.

THE MIGHTY RIGHT NOW GOD!!

Some folks say the Kingdom will be future, or

that the Kingdom was past, but some folks like to *live* in the future or the past. Yahweh, or Yah-vah, means 'The Mighty, **right now** God.' The Kingdom of God is past or future only to the extent that He was or will be King over something past or future. (And, absolutely He will be King over everything in the future—everything, Everything, EVERYTHING). Every church, every country, every people, every bank, every political party, every evangelistic association, every denomination, every mission board, every individual shall come under His Kingship or be destroyed. They will come under His rule willingly or unwillingly. "Every knee [shall] bow . . . , every tongue [shall] confess that Christ Jesus is LORD, to the glory of God the Father" Phil. 2:10, 11. "[All] the kingdoms of this world are become the [Kingdom] of our Lord, and of His Christ; and He shall reign for ever and ever" Rev. 11:15 (KJ).

This includes every financial kingdom, every religious, every business, every group, every individual kingdom—your kingdom too!

Rom. 14:17 says that the "Kingdom of God is . . . righteousness and peace and joy in the Holy Spirit." Do you like that word righteousness? Be honest. Righteousness means rightness—nitty gritty rightness—a right relationship with the King and the citizens of His Kingdom. But, more of this later.

I Corinthians 4:20 says that the Kingdom of

God consists of power. You'll see what kind of power. You'll either be a channel of it or a victim of it. You'll see just what is the Kingdom of God or the Kingdom of Heaven. Why, it's whatever God is the King of. If you and yours belong completely to the King and live the way He wants, then it's the Kingdom of God. But, if it's not, it's not.

Question: If you are going down the street and the Holy Spirit says, "Turn right," and you keep going straight, is Jesus being your Lord?

Question: If you have a wrong relationship to the King or the citizens of His Kingdom, are you a part of His Kingdom?

The Kingdom of God is what God is King of. Jesus says, "Not everyone that says to Me, 'Lord, Lord' will enter the Kingdom of Heaven, **but he that does the will of My Father** Who is in Heaven" Matt. 7:21. Are you one of those who call Him Lord, but do not do what He says???

Pray with me, please.

Lord Jesus, I make You King, Lord, and Master of all I am and have or ever will have or be. I choose You to be Lord over my possessions, business, family, future, money, my whole life. I give You everything, Everything, EVERYTHING!!! I give You all I am and all that I have and all that I shall ever have or be—**in exchange for** all You have and are. From now on, Lord God, I want what You want, Your perfect will, no matter what the cost!!! In Jesus' Name, Amen.

Review Questions

WHAT, WHEN & WHERE
IS THE KINGDOM OF GOD?!

1. What is the Kingdom of God? (Briefly)
2. Is the Kingdom of God past, present or future?
3. Even though Jesus told Pilate at the crucifixion, "My Kingdom is not of this world," where do the following scriptures indicate that God's Kingdom is? Psalm 47:7 _____; Jer. 10:7 _____; Rev. 2:26, 27 _____; Rev. 12:5 _____; Zech. 14:9 _____; Rev. 11:15 _____; Rev. 15:3, 4 _____.
4. What percentage would you say that God is King over: a. Your life? _____ b. Your family? _____ c. Your job? _____ d. Your possessions? _____ e. Your church? _____?
5. Would you say that you know the voice of the Lord?
6. According to Gal. 5, Eph. 5 and I Cor. 6, make a list of at least 15 kinds of people, or things that people do that will cause them to be excluded from the Kingdom of God.
7. According to Rev. 2:26, 27, who will have authority over the nations and who will rule them with a rod of iron?
8. List specifically some of the kinds of king-

doms that will either become the kingdoms of our Lord or be destroyed.

9. Make a guess (no answer will be provided by the teacher at this time) as to who the man-child is in Rev. 12:5.

10. What is the meaning of the word YAHVAH or YAHWEH?

11. What four things does Rom. 14:7 and I Cor. 4:20 say the Kingdom of God consists of?

12. Is Jesus being your Lord if you turn left when the Holy Spirit says "Go straight" or "Turn right"?

13. Is Jesus being your King if you have a wrong relationship to His subjects?

14. If you call Jesus your Lord, but don't do what the Father wants—will you inherit the Kingdom of God?

15. Will you give yourself to Jesus Christ now 100%? _____

16. Along with all that you own? _____ a. Or will ever own? _____ b. Or will ever have? _____ c. Or will ever be? _____

4

WHO IS THE KING?

My best research indicates that the word "Jehovah" was not ever used until about 1500 A.D. and then not by the Jewish people. It is an acronym—two words artificially joined together. The two words in this case appear to be the arbitrary, perhaps haphazard joining together of the vowels in the Hebrew Old Testament word for Almighty God, ADONAI, and the consonants of the Hebrew Old Testament word for God, used over 7000 times, YAHWEH, or YAHVAH, meaning "The Mighty Right Now God" or "The Great I Am That I Am" or "The Mighty God That Is He Who Is He Who Is" or "The God of the Present Moment." So, combining the vowels from YAHWEH, and the consonants from ADONAI they came up with Y or J,A,H,O,W or V,A,H or Jehovah. The dear Jehovah Witnesses should be calling Him YAHWEH or YAHVAH, and should be worshipping Him, Jesus Christ, God, as their

Right Now Saviour King. The Jehovah Witness' Bible does not even give the various names of God that the Hebrew gives. I wish I had a Bible that would give the following Hebrew names of God where they are much used in the Bible:

ELOHIM—Strong One. Gen. 1:1

EL—Strength, The Strong One.

ELAH or ALAH—To swear, to bind oneself by an oath, Faithfulness.

HAVAH—To become known, increasing self-revelation. Gen. 2:7

MELCHIZEDEK—Endless King of Righteousness. Gen. 14:18

EL ELYON—The Most High God, Possessor of Heaven and Earth.

EL SHADDAI—Almighty God, Satisfier, Nourisher, Strength-giver (Shad—woman's breast). Gen. 17:1

EL OLAM—Mysterious, Hidden, Everlasting God. Gen. 21:33

ADON, ADONI—Master, Husband. Gen. 15:2

ELYON—Highest.

EBENEEZER—Helper.

ISLI or ISHI—My Husband, My Man. Hosea 2:16

YAHWEH or YAHVAH—The Mighty Right Now God.

YAHWEH—SABBAOTH—War Lord of the Universe, or God of Hosts. I Sam. 1:3*

---

*Dawn Joy says, "God's Air Force."

YAHWEH—YIREH—The Lord Will Provide. Gen. 22:14

YAHWEH—RAPHAH—The Lord that Healeth. Ex. 15:26

YAHWEH—NISSI—The Lord Our Banner. Ex. 17:8-15

YAHWEH—SHALOM—The Lord Our Peace, or Send Peace. Judges 6:24

YAHWEH—RAAH—The Lord My Shepherd. Ps. 23

YAHWEH—TSIDKENU—The Lord Our Righteousness. Jer. 23:6

YAHWEH—SHAMMA—The Lord is Present. Ezekiel 48:35

YAHWEH—EL ROI—God of Vision. Gen. 16:13

YAH—(Abbreviation for Yahvah or Yahweh)

YAHWEH—ROPHEKA—

YAHWEH—MEQADDESHKEM—

YASHUA—YAVASHUA—Son of God, Saviour

QUANNA—Jealous. Ex. 34:14

IMMANUEL—God with us.

JESUS—SAVIOUR

SCRIPTURES ON GOD'S NAME

". . . to bring your sons from afar, their silver and their gold with them for the NAME OF THE LORD YOUR GOD. . ." Isa. 60:9. ". . . to make

THY NAME known to Thine adversaries. . ."
Isa. 64:2. "For THY NAME'S SAKE Thou wilt
lead me and guide me" Ps. 31:3b. "If you ask Me
anything IN MY NAME, I will do it." John
14:14. "Whatever you ask of the Father IN MY
NAME, He [will] give it to you." John 15:16.
There are literally hundreds and hundreds of
scriptures in both the Old and New Testament
that show without question that the Lord and
Saviour, Jesus Christ, the Messiah, is and shall
ever be the King of the Universe, the King of
Kings and the Lord of Lords. I'm reminded of
Psalm 2:12, "Do homage to the Son lest He become angry and you perish in the way. For His
wrath may soon [quickly, suddenly] be kindled.
How blessed are all who take refuge in Him."

Heavenly Father, I kiss Thy Son, the Messiah, the Lord Jesus Christ, the King of Kings,
the Lord of Lords. I receive Him as my Messiah,
Lord, Saviour, and my Life. In Jesus' Name,
Amen.

The writer has since discovered a few excellent sources on the Names of God! They are:

ROTHERHAM'S EMPHASISED BIBLE

The Newberry Bible, printed by Wyman &
Sons Ltd, 1959, London

The RESTORATION OF ORIGINAL SA-
CRED NAME BIBLE, 1976, Missionary Dispen-
sary Bible Research, P.O. Box 89, Winfield, Ala-
bama 35594

Lord Jesus Christ, Father God, please teach us about Your Name, how to ask "IN YOUR NAME," and how to always glorify Your Name. In Jesus' Name, Amen.

Review Questions

WHO IS THE KING?!

1. When was the word "Jehovah" probably first used?
2. Where did the name "Jehovah" probably come from?
3. What does the word YAHWEH or YAHVAH mean?
4. What necessary relationship with Yahweh do the Jehovah Witnesses and we need in order for them and us to enter into the Kingdom of God?
5. Define the following Names of God listed below:

Elohim _____

El _____

Elah or Alah _____

Havah _____

Melchizedek _____

El Elyon _____

El Shaddai _____

El Olam _____

Adon, Adonai _____

Elyon _____

Ebeneezer _____

Isli or Ishi _____

Immanuel _____

Yahweh or Yahvah _____

Yahweh-Rapha _____

Yahweh-Sabaoth _____

Yahweh-Yireh _____

Yahweh Nissi _____

Yahweh-Shalom _____

Yahweh-Raah _____

Yahweh-Tsidkenu _____

Yahweh-Shamma_____

Yahweh-El Roi _____

Yashua-Yavashua_____

Quanna _____

Jesus _____

5

HOW DO I JOIN THE KINGDOM OF GOD?

To become a member of the Kingdom of God is extremely simple or difficult, depending on one's perspective. It's easy if a person really wants to walk with God, difficult to the extent one does not. For example, Jesus said, "My yoke is *easy*, My burden is light." But "The way of the transgressor is *hard*," and "It is a *difficult* thing to kick against the ox goad." I've often told folks that if I were to swap all my theology for a totally selfish one, I wouldn't change a thing. Look at these promises from the Bible to a man that is in the will of God:

1. "Joy unspeakable and full of glory" I Pet. 1:8b (KJ)
2. "In Thy presence is fullness of joy; and at Thy right hand there are pleasures for evermore" Ps. 16:11 (KJ).
3. "Life . . . abundantly" John 10:10 (KJ).

4. "My joy . . . in you and your joy . . . full" John 15:11.
5. "[The overcomers] shall rule . . . over the nations . . . with a rod of iron" Rev. 2:26, 27 (KJ).
6. "God . . . giveth us richly all things to enjoy" I Tim. 6:17 (KJ).
7. "God . . . has blessed us with every spiritual blessing" Eph. 1:3.

—and infinitely more. Tell me, would you trade any of this for an eternity in hell? But it will cost you. Let's look again to see if the price is worth paying. Jesus Christ asked the question, "What will a man give in exchange for his own soul?" and "What will it profit a man if he gain the whole world and lose his own soul?" (Matt. 16:26; Mark 8:36; Luke 9:25)

Look at the positive side. You want to walk with God. Here's how: First, be born again. In John 3:3, 5, 7, Jesus promises that unless you are born again, you cannot see, or enter into, the Kingdom of God. Do you remember that religious painting where Jesus is standing outside the door of the cottage, knocking on the door? You'll see there's no latch on the outside. In Revelation 3:20 Jesus says, "Look, I'm standing at the door of your life and I'm knocking. If any of you will open the door of your life and invite Me to come in as your Saviour and Lord, I will come in and we'll have fantastic fellowship together"

(JB). You PRAY THIS PRAYER, "Lord Jesus Christ, I invite You to come into my life and be all that You are, in me. I give You my whole life. I admit that I have displeased You many times and have sinned. I receive Your whole Life in exchange for mine and receive You as my Salvation, my Lord, my Life, my Righteousness, etc. I ask You, Heavenly Father, to fill me with Your Holy Spirit of love Always. Thank You, Father for sending Thy Son, Jesus Christ, to take the penalty of my sins for me, by dying my death on the cross. I choose to obey You from now on, and to walk close to You, read Your Word, obey You and talk to You often. In Jesus' Name, Amen.

Feel better? You're on your way. John 1:12 is interesting. "But as many as *received* Him [Christ Jesus], to them [you] gave He the power to become the children of God, even to those who believe in His Name." So the potential to make it big in God is yours. Now, let's see how to make it happen.

Review Questions

HOW DO I JOIN
THE KINGDOM OF GOD?!

1. Explain what it means to be "born again"? (John 3:3, 5, 7)
2. How long have you been born again?
3. Who was instrumental in your new birth?
4. Why no latch on the outside of the door where Jesus is knocking?
5. If we open the door to our heart and invite Christ to come in, what will happen?
6. When Christ comes in, does He come in as Guest, Roomer, or Total Lord and Master of all the house?
7. How much does it cost to join the Kingdom of God?
8. List at least 12 things that we get in exchange.
9. Can we know that we are saved?
10. Who is our Salvation? (Not what, but Who?)
11. Is salvation a crisis or a process?
12. Does "Works" have anything to do with our salvation?
13. How many productive years do you think you have left before you stand before the Judgment Seat of Christ?

6

WHAT IS THE CITIZEN OF THE KINGDOM OF GOD?!!
or
HOW TO STAY IN THE KINGDOM OF GOD?!!!

The Word of God uses some of the following words to describe a Kingdom citizen: disciples, sons, friends, brothers of Christ, mothers and sisters of Christ. One must pay to become and remain a disciple or member or citizen of God's Kingdom. *The cost is:* **Everything you are and have in exchange for everything God has and is.** The only thing that's really required is that one become and do the will of the Lord. That's the Kingdom of God, simply doing and being what the King wants—the Lordship of Christ.

"As many as are led by the Spirit of God, they are the Sons of God." Rom. 8:14 (KJ). "Not every one that saith unto Me, Lord, Lord, shall enter into the Kingdom of heaven; but he that **doeth** the will of My Father which is in heaven. Many will say to Me in that day, Lord, Lord, have we not prophesied in Thy name? and in Thy Name have cast out devils? and in Thy name done many wonderful works? And then I will profess unto them, I never knew you: depart from Me, ye that work iniquity" Matt. 7:21-23 (KJ). Jesus asked, "Why call ye Me Lord, Lord, and do not the things which I say?" Luke 6:46 (KJ). Dear one, **it's not enough** to claim to be saved or born again or Spirit filled or a church member or anything, if you claim Christ Jesus as your Lord but do not do what He wants or says.

A citizen of the kingdom of God is one who (is born again, but who also) does what the King of kings, the Lord Jesus Christ, wants. Let's look at three verses in Luke 14 regarding those who **cannot** be a Kingdom citizen: Large crowds were traveling with Jesus, and turning to them He said: "If anyone comes to Me and does not hate his own father and mother, and wife and children, and brothers and sisters—yes, and even his own life—he **cannot be My disciple**" Luke 14:26-27. What this means simply is that **the will of God must come first**—ahead of the will, wishes, desires, threats, opinions, commands, or intimidations of your parents, children, spouse, friends, enemies, church members, and those whose opinions you respect the most. **Most of all**, the will and desire of God must surely be more important to you than your own will or desire.

You MUST carry your cross! But remember Jesus said, "My yoke is easy and My burden is light" Matt. 11:30 (KJ). Which do you choose— your yoke or Satan's yoke, your burden, your friend's burden, or Christ's easy yoke, His light burden? Luke 14:33, "So therefore, **no one of you can be my disciple who does not give up all his own possessions**"!!! If you want to be His disciple, then you must give up ownership and legal title to **everything** you own—give it to the King of the Kingdom, Jesus Christ and the Father, so that He retains title and ownership to ALL that you have and are! your life! your will! your time! your worship! your children! your spouse! your money! your future! your possessions! your opinions! your plans! your reputation! your career! your sins! your ideas! your religious ruts! your stubbornness! **yourself**! Unless you are willing to forsake **all** of these things you **cannot** be His disciple!!! It's impossible for you to have Christ Jesus as your Lord and do not **do** what He wants!!! The Kingdom of God is what God is King of. And if God is not allowed to be your Absolute Master or your King in some area of your life, then it's not the Kingdom of God and you are **not** His brother or disciple or Kingdom citizen or friend. "Ye are My friends IF ye do whatsoever I command you" John 15:14, and, "Why call ye Me, Lord, Lord, and do not the things which I say?"! Luke 6:46 (KJ).

Jesus said, "**not** everyone that saith unto Me,

Lord, Lord, shall enter into the Kingdom of
Heaven; but he that **doeth** the will of My Father
which is in heaven" Matt. 7:21 (see above). Perhaps you are thinking, "This is impossible." Do
you remember Matthew 19:23-26? "Jesus said to
His disciples, 'Truly I say to you,' [or 'I tell you
the truth'], 'it is hard for a rich man to enter the
Kingdom of Heaven.' [It still is] 'Again I say to
you, it is easier for a camel to go through the eye
of a needle than for a rich man to enter the Kingdom of God.' [Think about that!] And when the
disciples heard this, they were very astonished
and said, 'Then who can be saved?' Jesus [looked
at them and] said, 'With men this is impossible,
but **with God all things are possible.**' "

What about it, amigo? Do you want to change
the scriptures to mean, "With God **some** things
are possible"? "My God will supply **some** of my
needs"? "I can do **some** things through Christ"?
But we here are only fulfilling the Great Commission when we are teaching you to obey **"all
things whatsoever** I [Jesus] have commanded
you" Matt. 28:20 (KJ).

Lord, I repent of my unbelief. I choose to believe in You. I not only seek Your Kingdom first,
but also I seek Your righteousness. Teach me,
Lord Jesus, what seeking first Your righteousness
is. In Jesus' Name. Amen. . . . And by the way
Lord, I now hereby give You Everything I have
and am: my life, my will, my time, my worship,
my children, my spouse, my money, my future,

my possessions, my opinions, my plans, my reputation, my career, my sins, my ideas, my religious ruts, my stubbornness, my self and everything I ever will have or be—**now**! for all time—I give it all to You, forever. In Jesus' Name, Amen!!!!

Review Questions

WHAT IS THE CITIZEN OF THE KINGDOM OF GOD?!

1. What is the first thing necessary to become a citizen of the Kingdom of God?
2. Give at least 4 synonyms the Lord gives for a Kingdom citizen.
3. What one single characteristic marks or identifies a born again citizen of the Kingdom of God?
4. How much does it cost to be a citizen of the Kingdom of God?
5. Is it possible to claim Jesus as Lord and still not inherit the Kingdom of God? (Read Rom. 8:14; Matt. 7:21-23; Lk. 6:46 and write them down.)
6. What two groups of people did Jesus say cannot be His disciples? (Lk. 14:26-27)
7. Lk. 14:33 says who else cannot be Christ's disciple?
8. What general and specific things are you willing to give to Him now 100%? (List at least 30 things.)
9. What generally and specifically are you willing to DO for the Lord Jesus Christ? (List at least 30 things.)
10. What generally and specifically are you willing to BE for the Lord Jesus Christ? (List at least 12 things.)

11. If you are not Christ's disciple—then whose disciple are you?

12. Will it be harder or more difficult to be Christ's disciple or the devil's? (Guess) Rom. 8:18, Prov. 13:15, Matt. 11:28-29.

13. What of ours did Christ take with Him to the cross? (Name at least 3 of the most important things.)

14. Is it necessary for us to "feel" saved before we are?

7

THE KING'S GREATEST SECRET
or
HOW TO BE PERFECT

God has a Secret!!! He would like to tell it to You! The angels and men of God wanted to know this Secret, but God wouldn't tell them for thousands of years. Then God told The Secret to the church through the Apostle Paul and the other apostles and prophets. That Secret was lost and forgotten again during the Dark Ages, but now is being told again in this special time to the church. It's the King's Greatest Secret! It needs to be told so very much. Almost no one in the Church today knows The Secret. We have ministered in many churches across the country and in most of them we ask a certain question to find out if they know The Secret. And in none of the places where we have ministered have they known. The question we asked them was, "What did Jesus take of ours with Him to the cross?" Will you take a minute to answer this before you continue?

We get answers, all of them correct but not complete, like "He took our sins, our sicknesses, our burdens, etc." We say, "That's true that He took these so we can be forgiven, healthy, and without worry (some folks cast their burdens upon Yahweh, the Mighty Right **now** God, but as a fisherman casts, they sit and reel these burdens back to themselves). But the people still have not told the main thing Christ took with Him to the cross! I suppose the reason they do not know is that it requires a revelation of God, or one who has a revelation from God to share The Secret, before they can know. What a Wonderful Mystery!

The Secret is found in plain sight in a multitude of places in the Bible, especially in places like John 17, Ephesians, Romans, Galatians, Colossians, etc. The Secret Mystery is this: When Christ went to the cross, He took **us** with Him there! When He died, **we** died! When He was buried, **we** were buried with **all** of our insufficiencies, inadequacies, inferiorities, insecurities, inabilities, and instabilities!!!! Everything negative or nasty or weak or sinful about us He took to the cross, because He took **us** to the cross. Oh, dear one, if you grasp hold of this Secret it will make all the difference between Christ living your life, and you living your life; between you trying to speak good things, and Christ speaking His words through you.

Lord Jesus, please make this plain and understandable. We believe together that You will

make the Mystery clear. "I praise Thee, O
Father, Lord of heaven and earth, that Thou
didst hide these things from the wise and intelli-
gent, and didst reveal them to babes. Yes,
Father, for thus it was well pleasing in Thy sight"
Matt. 11:25 and Luke 10:21.

Please let me tell you more about The Secret.
When The Lord Jesus Christ went to the cross He
took you with Him there! **You were there** when
they crucified my Lord! Christ looked ahead into
time and saw you and decided that He could not
help you any other way, that He could not beat or
bless you into being what He wants you to be,
could not educate or "religious" you adequately,
but that the only hope for you was to take you
with Him to the Cross and kill you dead, along
with all of your negative nature and qualities,
and bury you.

Unlike many self-help books, Christ does not
try to get you to "hype" or hypnotize, con or convince yourself into thinking that you are really
good or nice, adequate or o.k., but that you are
totally hopeless and helpless apart from Christ
taking you to the cross with Him and putting all
of your self to death and burying it in the tomb
with Him. So you do not need to kill yourself or
commit suicide, nor do your friends, because
Jesus Christ lovingly killed us softly already. But
that is not the end of the story!

When Christ rose from the tomb **He raised us up** as a whole, new, beautiful, wonderful, adequate, sufficient, glorious, superior, perfect, secure creation in His image in newness of Life so He could come into us and **be** our Life, Live our Life, **be** our perfection, **be** our righteousness!!!

Perhaps you would like to see this Secret in the scriptures. The following verses can become attainable in the practical realm of the nitty gritty now:

I Cor. 15:57	Victory
II Cor. 2:14-16	Victory always everywhere
Rom. 6:7, 18, 22	Free from sin
Col. 3:1-3	Risen with Christ our life
Eph. 2:6	Seated in Christ
Ps. 16:11	Fullness of joy; joy unspeakable
Eph. 1:3, 4	Every blessing
Ne. 8:10	Joy of the Lord—strength
I Cor. 2:16	Mind of Christ
Ph. 4:13	Can do all things through Christ
Jude 24	Walk blamelessly
Matt. 28:18	All power and authority
Matt. 5:14	We are the light of the World
Ph. 1:21	To Live Is Christ
II Cor. 9:8	All power and authority

John 14:13	Whatever we ask
John 10:10	Abundant life
II Pet. 1:1-4	We have all things for life
Rom. 8:37	More than conquerors
I John 4:17	We are as He is
Matt. 19:26	All things are possible with.
I John 2:6	We can walk as He walked
John 14:12	Greater works
Luke 8:10	We can know the mysteries of the Kingdom of God
Col. 1:25-29	Mystery of the gospel of the ages
I Cor. 1:30	Christ is made unto us Wisdom, Righteousness, Sanctification and Redemption

Galatians 2:20 says, "I *have been* crucified *with* Christ, and it is no longer I who live, **but Christ lives in me!!!**" In Colossians, God says that **Christ is our life!** The Bible says, "For me to live IS Christ" (Phil. 1:21), and "We **have** the mind of Christ" (I Cor. 2:16), and "*As He* [Christ] *is* **so are we in this world**" I John 4:17. Oh, dear heart, I pray for you with deep, unutterable longing and faith "That the God of our Lord Jesus Christ, the Father of Glory, may give you a spirit of wisdom and of revelation in the knowledge of Him! I pray that the eyes of your heart may be enlightened so that you may **know**. . ." Eph. 1:17, 18.

HOW TO BE PERFECT

You simply know and **"reckon yourself to have been crucified with Christ"** (Rom. 6:6), and **then consider and reckon yourself as "dead indeed unto sin, self and satan,** but alive unto God through Jesus Christ our Lord!!! (Rom. 6:11) **Allelujaweh!!!** Thank you, Dear Lord Jesus, for taking us to the cross with You and for raising us up with You in newness of Life in You. Lord God, we receive You to be *all that You are, in us,* now and forever more. Amen. Jesus said, **"Be ye therefore perfect, even as your Father in heaven is perfect."** Matt. 5:48. Jesus, as always, meant just what He said! He meant, **"Be as perfect as God!"** Or would you prostitute and change and twist and warp and non-effectualize the Word of God here or any other place?

It does **not** mean "try to be perfect" nor "be perfect sometime after your body has rotted," nor "give up on being perfect," nor "it's impossible to be perfect," nor "wish that you were perfect," nor "God isn't great enough to make or keep me perfect," nor "be theoretically perfect," nor any of that kind of silliness. 'Would be' disciples of the Kingdom, **won't be** disciples of the Kingdom of God as long as they are messing with the commands of the King of God's Kingdom in this way! One who changes the commands of the King is a Kingdom Anarchist and traitor. When someone asks, "What does this verse mean?" the best answer is, "The Bible means what it says!" because the King means what He says. I believe that whenever there is a disagreement about a scripture, it is because one or more of them is not willing to accept what the scripture and King says.

THE GREATEST MOMENT OF MY LIFE

One day Patty Troug at Bethel College told me, "John, as long as you are calling 'idealistic,' 'unattainable,' or 'theoretical' what God calls necessary, practical, available, and attainable, **you** are calling God a **liar!!!** I had thrown a book away from me in disgust, *Forever Triumphant*, by Huegel, in which he quoted II Corinthians 2:14, "Thanks be unto God who in Christ **always** causes us to triumph and manifests Christ through us in **every** place!" (JB) Victory, at **all** times and in every place! I had said "that's too idealistic," but then I realized, as a result of Patricia's gentle rebuke, that I had been calling God a liar in that He had said, "Victory always and everywhere." And I had said, "Impossible." I did not want to call God a liar anymore, so I went to my room, got out my Bibles, KJV, AMP, Gdspd, Greek N.T., etc., and laid them out on Bruce Leafblad's vacant bunk, to see just what God **did** say. Sure enough, God said, "Perfect victory always" and "More than conquerors" and "Abundant Life" and "Joy unspeakable" and "Full of Glory" and "WE have the Mind of

Christ" and "Christ our Life" and "whatever we ask" and "Greater works than these shall ye do" and "I can do all things through Christ" and "With God all things are possible" etc., etc., etc., etc. *All these Bibles* said the same thing, so I decided to do three things:

1. Confess every known sin, including having called God a liar;
2. Yield myself **completely** to the Lord Jesus Christ.

I told the Lord Jesus that I would be willing to be sick, maimed, killed, single, celibate, persecuted, misunderstood, forgotten, married to anyone He said (I was sure He was going to make me marry somebody really terrible). Anyway, I really meant business.

Now, these first two steps I had taken many times before, but I took them again. In fact, we should always keep up to date with the Lord, staying free from sin and staying in a totally yielded state.

3. Appropriate by faith the highest level walk in God's Spirit, with Christ AS your Life! Invite Jesus Christ to come into your life and take over completely as Saviour, Lord and Life!!!

Charles Trumble, in *The Life That Wins,**

*From *The Life That Wins* or *Victory In Christ,* Christian Literature Crusade, Fort Washington, Pennsylvania, 19034.

says that on this third step of faith, everything now depends. He suggested that we take a step of faith with total disregard for the presence or lack of accompanying signs or proofs, because the transaction must be based on faith rather than some feeling or tingle, etc. So, I remember reaching out my hand to the Lord God and saying, "Lord Jesus, I believe You have a walk for me that I haven't been experiencing; a relationship and an experience with You that I haven't had before. Lord Jesus, I don't know what to call it, and I don't know how to get it, but whatever You call it and however one gets it, I receive it from You now in cold, blind faith, not depending on outward feelings or 'signs' as the proof of the transaction. Thank You very much. In Jesus' Name, Amen."

Can you guess what happened? You guessed it. Nothing. Outwardly, or on a feeling level, that is. I felt really dead. Oh, I had accepted the Lord Jesus as my personal Saviour many years before, and I had yielded my Life to Him many times before. But the same thing had happened to me as would have happened in the Old Testament if one would have taken a clean lamb of the flock without blemish and then sacrificed the lamb under the hot Israel sun . . . and that's all. Can you imagine the mess? The sacrifice needed the fire of God to come from heaven to light upon and consume the sacrifice as a sign of acceptance and anointing. But I rose from my knees there at

Gerald Healy's house where Bruce Leafblad and I were renting while attending Bethel College, November 1960, my senior year. I put away all my Bibles and climbed wearily into my top bunk. After I was settled down, I thought, "If anybody asked me to praise the Lord right now, it would be like someone asking me to praise a haystack." I suppose I was remembering a time when I had gone to visit a church and had tried to get "ba'tzd wi' d' HoliGoz' " and the pastor was on one side telling me to say "Prayz Gawd" just as loud as I could, whilst the preacher's wife was on the other side, encouraging me to say, "How'-lay-lew'yuh" just as fast as I could. I recall how terribly difficult it had been to say either one either way. Folks who know me now are surprised that I didn't bound out of my mother's womb shouting "How'lay-lew'ya." One time, at Bible School, a staff member said the reason John Bohlen praised the Lord was because he had a 'sanguine' personality. I told her, "Yes, Joyce, the 47th Psalm says, 'O clap your hands, [all ye **sanguines**], shout unto God with the voice of triumph'!!!" By the way, that's not quite how it reads—it reads **'all ye people.'** So it's not just those with an enthusiastic personality that are to beautifully and enthusiastically and constantly worship the Lord: **all** of us are.!!!

CATACLYSMIC REVOLUTION

Anyway, no sooner had that thought crossed my mind about praising a haystack, (indicating the lacking emotional level of positive feeling) when Christ became my Life!, and I have never been the same since. It seemed like a great dam broke on the inside and there came explosively gushing over me, and through me, and to me, and from me, and upon me, and around me, from deep within and from high above came the Glory of God, and the Joy of God, and the Love of God, and the Spirit of God, and the **Life** of God, and the Peace of God, and the Presence of God, and the Strength of God, and the Anointing of God, and the Overflowing, Effervescent Flooding Fullness of the Living God!!! I have never been the same! Fabulous! Incredible! Joyful! Invigorating! Beautiful! Astounding! Healing! Wonderful! Marvelous! Lasting! Satisfying! Miraculous! Life-changing! Christ became my Life! I saw myself as having been crucified with Christ, dead and buried with Christ, risen with Christ Jesus in newness of Life, and seated in Christ at the Father's right hand, far over and above everything that is named in heaven and on earth, and glorified in Him, Jesus Christ. This is described in Eph. 2, and Col. 3, Rom. 6, and Rom. 8, Eph. 3, II Cor. 3, etc., etc., etc., etc.

From the Amplified Bible, Eph. 3:19b—"That you may be filled (through all your being) unto *all the fullness of God*—[that is], may have the **richest** measure of the Divine presence, and become a body **wholly** filled and flooded with God Himself."

"The question for all of us, *no matter what our*

theological background is: **Are you filled with God right now? Jesus said, "He that believes Me, out of his innermost being shall gush forth flooding torrents of Living Water continuously." John 7:38 (JB-ANT)**

Question—Are you full of God and His Holy Spirit right *this moment?* **Are you up to date with Him and on excellent terms with Him** *right now?* **Do you minister and share from the overflow, or are you like a "small handful of water in a big empty barrel?" Pray with me.**

Dear Father God, thank You for providing unlimited anointing and every blessing, and having "given us all things that pertain to life and godliness." I ask You to **be** my life; be **all** that You **are,** in me from now on. I reckon and consider the old to be dead. I receive You as my "Wisdom, Righteousness, Sanctification, and Redemption." Be my Perfection. Love through me, speak Your Words Through me, pray through me. Thank You, Mighty Right Now God. I believe from now on I can do **all** things through Christ my Life, and that nothing shall be impossible IN **You.** In Jesus' Name, Amen.

We can have an experience *more real* than if we fell dead, and Christ was looking around for a freshly dead warm body in which to live, that He could come into and **be** the **life** of, that He could live His divine glorious life through!!!

He's coming in the clouds—don't mistake that, and "Every eye shall see Him", but He also wants to be glorified and magnified now **in** all who believe!! "When He shall come to be glorified **in** His saints and to be admired **in** all them that believe, (because our testimony among you was believed) in that day" II Th. 1:10 (KJ).

So, back to the illustration—Say that Christ came into your available dead body and **became** its **life**, that is, started living His Glorious Life through you, loving through you, talking, walking, living, loving, blessing, healing, being all that He is—in you—being your Salvation, **not** giving you Salvation as an experience **apart** from Him.

I Corinthians 1:30 says that Christ, "**is made unto us Wisdom, and Righteousness, and Sanctification, and Redemption.**" These things: Resurrection, Salvation, etc., are not a "thing", or an "experience" apart from Him, but are a **Person.** That Person's Name is **Yahvah or Yahweh,** The Mighty Right Now God, The Lord and Saviour Jesus Christ!!!

But you don't need to die or commit suicide—because Christ wants to become your life by your acceptance. Accept what He did when He took **not only** our sins and sicknesses, so we can be forgiven and healed completely, but He took our selves. Rom. 6, Col., Eph., etc. He killed **us** with all of our insufficiencies, inadequacies, inferiorities, inabilities, instabilities, and took us to the cross, put us to death, buried us and raised us up in newness of life, a whole, new, beautiful, glorious, adequate, sufficient, wonderful, creation fashioned in His image, that He wants to **be** the life of.

The story is told of an elephant that had a friend who was a flea that rode around behind his ear. One day they crossed a jungle bridge that shook, and swung and swayed. After crossing the bridge, the flea whispered into the elephant's ear, "We sure shook that bridge didn't we!!" And at the end of the day you can whisper into the Ear of God, your Friend, "We sure shook our world today, didn't we?"

This will come as a surprise to many, but Christ is **not** interested in **helping** you to be righteous, or wise, or strong, or alive, apart or distant from Himself. He wants to **be** your Righteousness, **be** your Wisdom, **be** your Strength, **be** your Life, **be** your Everything. He doesn't want to **help** you say good words, or pray, or be disciplined, or heal, or bless, or love, as something distant or apart from Himself. He wants to pray His prayers through you by the Holy Spirit, to say His words through you, to bless with His blessing through you, to heal with His Healing through you, to love with His love through you. Do you see the difference?

So, we can have an experience *greater* than if we had a heart attack and Jesus Christ came into our newly dead body and started living in the earth disguised *as us,* because *better than this* **can be ours** by accepting that He killed us already on the cross in order to do this very thing! Now He wants to BE all that He is in us, BE our life, etc., and if Christ IS our righteousness, we'll be as righteous as the Father, because the Righteousness He manifests through us will be as righteous as the Father's! Remember Jesus said in Matthew 5:48—**"Be ye therefore perfect even as your Father in heaven is perfect."** That's how we do it. Simply reckon the old life to be dead (Rom. 6), and receive Christ, not only inside to **be** your Saviour and Master and total Lord, but also **being** all that He is, in you, as your Life!!!

He wants to walk around in your shoes, wearing your clothes, speaking **His** words, praying **His** prayers, thinking **His** thoughts, blessing **His** people, loving, healing through you. He wants to **be** the Parent of your children, **be** the Spouse of your mate, **be** the Worker on your job, **be** the Child of your parents, **be** the Friend of your friends, **be** the Leader in your church, the Leader in your community, the Changer of your world, the Establisher of His Kingdom, the Binder and Looser of situations, the Fulfiller of the Great Commission, and of **all** His commandments, **in you** and **through you!!!** (Matt. 28:18-20, I John 2). **All this can be ours from now on as Christ is our life!!** (I John 4:17). **Amen!!!!!!!**

Christ wants there to be **no difference** between who He is at the right hand of the Father and who He is—**in us!!!!!** Amen!!! The Bible says, "The very same image." "As He is so are we in this world." "In His image."

If you have any question about this, get in touch with us—because this **must** become absolutely clear to you, absolutely workable! It's the Key literally to **everything** you are in God.

Here it is then—God's Greatest Secret!!! Christ living His Glorified Life in you as your Life!!! **Christ living His glorified life in you—in me—as our glorified life!!!** "For me to live is Christ." "I live—yet not I, but Christ." This chapter—this concept—these truths—are the most important thing in this book! If I only have a chance to tell people one thing, I tell them this. The vast majority of Christians, (I would say more than 99%), do not have a working knowledge of this Greatest Secret of God! I believe that the need is so great for people to know this truth, that if you and I dedicated the rest of our entire lives to sharing this one truth it would be worthwhile! What is your life being dedicated to at the present time anyway?

What would happen if Christ came to the earth to live in disguise in someone before His coming in the clouds? What if He came to live His glorified Life in Your town? Your family? Your church? Your factory? Your marriage? Your shoes? Well, that's exactly what Christ wants to happen!!! Exactly! **No difference.**

Please now let us make a prayer of II Thessalonians 1:10, "Lord God of the impossible, now and ever, please now come and be made all glorious in me and be marvelled at in me. I believe, Lord God, I believe, for You to live Your life—**in me**. Yea, **be** my Life! I reckon my old life to be crucified! dead! and buried! I consider my New Life to be risen! ascended! seated! glorified! and reigning! in You, and You in me—Right Now! In **this** world! In **my** life! **AS My Life! From now on! And to tell this Secret to as many as possible! As quickly as possible! By whatever means possible! In Jesus' Name, Amen!!**

Now, let's look at one of the things that might happen if your friend learns this Secret.

Review Questions

THE KING'S GREATEST SECRET

1. Is it possible to live without sinning? (explain)
2. What of ours did Christ take with Him to the cross?
3. What is God's greatest secret?
4. What is the difference between Christ helping you do or speak good things and Him speaking or doing good things through you?
5. Why was it necessary for Christ to take you with Him to the cross?
6. If Christ did not take you to the cross, and you don't know it—has positive thinking got much power?
7. Why is suicide not necessary?
8. The following phrases go with what scripture verse (you may look them up from the list of scriptures provided below): Victory _____ , Victory always everywhere _____, Free from sin _____, Risen with Christ our life _____, Seated in Christ _____, Fullness of joy: joy unspeakable _____, Every blessing _____, Joy of the Lord _____, strength _____ , Mind of Christ _____, Can do all things through Christ _____ , Walk blamelessly _____ , All power and authority _____, We are

the light of the World _____, To live is
Christ _____ , All power and authority
_____ , Whatever we ask _____ ,
Abundant Life _____ , We have all
things for life _____ , More than con-
querors _____ , We can be as He is
_____ , All things are possible
_____ , We can walk as He walked
_____, Greater works _____ , We
can know the mysteries of the kingdom of
God _____ , Mystery of the gospel of the
ages _____, Christ is made unto us wis-
dom _____.

Jude 24; Ph. 1:21; Eph. 1:3, 4; Rom 8:37; Col.
3:1-3; II Cor. 2:14-16; Matt. 5:14; II Pet.
1:1-4; John 14:13; Ps. 16:11; Rom. 6:7, 18, 22;
Ph. 4:13; Ne. 8:10; Eph 2:6; I Cor. 15:57; I
Cor. 2:16; Matt. 28:18; II Cor. 9:8; I Cor.
1:30; Luke 8:10; I John 4:17; John 10:10;
John 14:12; Matt. 19:26; Col. 1:25-29; I John
2:6.

9. Gal. 2:20—Are you living?
10. Can we be perfect?
11. What did Jesus mean when He said be per-
    fect? (Matt. 5:48)
12. How can we be perfect?
13. What is the main solution for most argu-
    ments about the Bible?
14. How is calling "idealistic" what God calls
    necessary and practical—calling God a liar?
15. What 3 steps are necessary for Christ to be
    your life?
16. Do you have the mind of Christ?

17. In the Word, what's the main evidence, sign, fruit, or proof that you are full of God?

18. Not "have" you been filled with, but are you full of God right now? (Give yourself a percentage)

19. What would happen to a clean and freshly sacrificed (killed) lamb under the hot Israel sun if nothing more happened after it was killed?

20. What else is necessary?

21. What is this symbolic of?

22. Who should praise the Lord with shouting and clapping? (Ps. 47)

23. Why can we have an experience MORE REAL than if we fell dead and Christ was looking around for a fresh warm dead body He could move into and raise up and become the Life of, living on the earth again—disguised as you?

24. Who is the flea—the elephant in the illustration?

25. What is the main difference between Christ *helping* us do or be something, and Him being or doing it in and through us?

26. Can we be perfect? If so, how?

27. Does Christ want there to be any difference between who He is at the Father's right hand and who He is—in us?

28. If you devoted the rest of your life to sharing this secret—would your life be well spent?

29. Will you?

Chris Wold Dyrud

8

WHEN DID I TOUCH THE KING?
or
ARE YOU A HAWG WALLER WALLERER?
or
DO YOU LIKE HAWG WALLERS?
or
KINGDOM ANARCHY, SEDITION, AND INSURRECTION

One day, while interceding for Minneapolis and St. Paul, I received a "visionette" which I believe is from the Lord. You will be able to picture it with me. I could see two hills beside one another with a tree in the foreground and a path coming down off the hill past a 'hog-waller' by the tree. Do you know what a hog-waller is? Well, a hog-waller is a mud hole what hogs like to 'waller' in. Well, down this here path come, guess what? you guessed it. A hawg! And can you guess what this here **purty** pink hog did when it got to the mud hole? You guessed it! Jumped right in, he did (I think it was a he. A feller wouldn't hardly think a lady gender would like hog-wallers that much). Well, just about that time a bee-yeautiful, fluffy, snow white kitty cat come a tippy toein' it down the path, and can you guess what that there cat done when it got to the mud hole? Well, believe it or not, that cat jumped scat into that mud hole and started to havin' a happy time. Next, down the path come a Be-you-too-full little baby lamb, whose fleece was white as snow, Lo, behold and consternation, (I wonder how you guessed it) that there little, pure white lamb jumped in that hog-waller and started to havin' a happy time. Why from the way it was actin' you'da thunk it was a mutton head! I asked the Lord, "Lord, what are You trying to show me?" And it seemed as though the Lord said, "The mud hole represents anarchy of the Kingdom of God, or Kingdom rebellion, sedition, arrogance, belligerence, defiance, hostility, mutiny, anarchy, treachery, insurrection, treason, insubordination, stubbornness, etc. The pig represents natural man, with his natural propensity for such things; the kitten represents religious man; and the lamb represents spiritual people." Whereupon I said, "Yes, but it's against the nature of a kitten and a lamb to like mud." It seemed as though the Lord said, "It's also contrary to the nature of spiritual and religious people to like rebellion, anarchy, sedition, mutiny, defiance, belligerence, hostility, arrogance, treachery, insurrection, insubordination, treason, and stubbornness." Then it seemed as though the Lord Jesus began to show me what He has been putting up with. I could visualize a person with his hand stretched to the Lord, saying, "Lord Jesus, I love You, but I refuse to accept this one whom You send," or, "I love You, God, but I'll not accept what You have to say to me through this one or that one."

We have defined Kingdom anarchy as being: **"Any one or any thing that rejects or fails to cooperate with anyone the King sends or anything that the King directs or desires."**

THEOCRACY vs DEMOCRACY

The American way of life has its roots in words like "Independence", "Democracy", "Freedom" and a whole mess of words that begin with self: Self-initiative, self-confidence, self-assertion, etc. But the King of God's Kingdom calls for a death to self that puts Christ Jesus the Creator King of all the universe on the throne. All the trouble in the world—directly or indirectly— relates to the increasing conflict between self will and the will of God. Thus, the gospel of the Kingdom of God runs directly cross grain to every kingdom—personal, religious, political, financial—that to whatever extent fails to conform to the wishes of the King of all the universe. Many Christians and Christian organizations may be understandably "threatened" that are calling Christ Lord but are not doing what Christ as Lord wants. But make no mistake! The whole of scripture indicates that Christ the Creator King is taking over. Revelation 15:11 and a host of other scriptures indicate that God is establishing a Theocracy—or a government run by God—in the earth. This will not be a democracy. But we will get to vote—for God's total authority over everything—or . . . well, exclusion from God's Kingdom. Read it. "Not everyone who says to Me, Lord, Lord, will enter the Kingdom of heaven, but he who does the will of My Father who is in heaven." *Luke 7:21 ANT. & Psalm 2: "Kiss the son, lest He be angry & ye perish from the way."*

Many people and organizations may become angry or threatened with this because of their arrogance, own-wayness, tradition, habits, independence, selfishness "rutualism", etc. But make no mistake—the Lordship and Kingship of Christ takes the priority—and Christ will be King over all.

We have no right to run our churches—or our businesses, or our family, or our finances, or our time, talents, professions, resources—the way we are used to running them if to whatever extent they fail to conform to the will of the King.

YOU DID IT TO ME!!!

Remember the story of the excited woman who had been promised a visit at her house from the King in person? When only a child, a poor beggar and an old man appeared during that day, she was disappointed and next day asked the King why He did not come. He said, "I did come, but I was disguised as a child, a poor beggar, and an old man . . . and do you remember how you received Me?"

Consider the following scriptural examples of Kingdom Anarchy:

1. Matt. 10:40, "He who receives you receives Me, and he who receives Me receives Him who sent Me." *verse 41,* "He who receives a prophet in the name of a prophet shall receive a prophet's reward." The question I have is, **"What happens if** we reject the prophet or reject the righteous man, or refuse to give to one of the little ones a cup of cold water, or refuse to give to our Kingdom brother that asks of us"??? And now the rest of verses 41 and 42, " . . . and he who receives a righteous man in the name of a righteous man shall receive a righteous man's reward. And whoever in the name of a disciple gives to one of these little ones [or humble folk] even a cup of cold water to drink, truly I say to you he shall not lose his reward."

2. Luke 10:16, "The one who listens to you listens to Me, and the one who rejects you rejects

Me; and he who rejects Me rejects the One who sent Me." How about putting this in our promise box and our memory pack? And how about putting our brother or sister *who is doing the will of God,* in the verse? It would (and in truth does) read like this, "The one who listens to [them] listens to Me, and the one who rejects [them] rejects Me; and he who rejects Me. . ." Or apply this verse to yourself and make it read like this (because it does): "If I reject the representatives of Jesus, those who are doing the will of God in the Spirit of God in the Love of God, then I am rejecting Jesus Christ Himself, and if I listen to the representatives of Jesus Christ, then I am listening to Christ Himself." Or is that too strong? I'll leave the decision to you, and your decision will be put to the test of fire at the Judgment Seat of God. But before you hurry on, go back and read the verse again in your favorite translation! (Remember, our definition of **a Kingdom Representative is anyone the King has commissioned to represent Him in any regard**—but we are not talking about "professional" men of God, or religious men—but those **who are totally committed to the will of God and are lovingly functioning under His Lordship and His leading!!**)

3. The sheep and the goats: "Then the King will say to those on His right, 'Come, you who are blessed of my Father, inherit the Kingdom

prepared for you from the foundation of the world" (Matt. 25:34). These got into the Kingdom of God because they gave food, clothing, and shelter to those who are doing the Father's will! "And the King will answer and say to them, Truly, I say to you, to the extent that you did it to one of these brothers of Mine, even the least of them, you did it **to Me!!**" (Matt. 25:40) The reason the others went to hell's "eternal fire" was because they did **not** give food, clothing, and shelter to those who *were doing the will of God.* "Then He will answer them, saying, Truly, I say to you, to the extent that you did not do it to one of the least of these, you did not do it **to Me!!!** And these will go away into eternal punishment, but the righteous into eternal life" (Matt. 12:45-46). Perhaps you may be asking, "To whom does 'the least of these My brothers' refer?" Jesus Himself answered that question in Matthew 12:46-50, "While He was still speaking to the multitudes, behold, His mother and His brothers were standing outside, seeking to speak to Him. And someone said to Him, 'Behold, your mother and your brothers are standing outside seeking to speak to You.' But He answered the one who was telling Him and said, 'Who is My mother and who are My brothers?' And stretching out His hand toward His disciples, He said, 'Behold, My mother and My brothers! For **whoever**

shall do the will of My Father who is in heaven, he **is My brother and sister and mother'.''**Also in Luke 8:20, 21, "But He (Jesus) answered and said unto them, 'My mother and My brothers are **these who hear the word of God and do it.'** "

It is interesting to see what things anger certain people. For example, in our presenting the Gospel of the Kingdom to the dear ones, some folks have become angry with us at this point. One dear man said, "Now, just wait a minute here, John, it sounds to me like you are saying that I've got to receive you and your message, and that seems too dogmatic for me!" To which I responded, "Jim, I'm perfectly willing not to be an issue here, but let me ask you one question." He said, "O.K." So I said, "suppose there was a man sent from God whose name was uh, Don or George, and that he was commissioned from God and that he had a message from God, that he is one of the 12 or the 70 that Christ sent out; and that uh, George and Don, as perfect strangers, come to town and that they are not received. What would happen to those dear folks who rejected uh, George or Don? Won't it be true of them that 'it will be more tolerable for the land of Sodom and Gomorrah in the day of judgment, than for that city [or group or person rejecting]??' " (Matt. 10:15). Jim agreed. And whether or not you and I agree on this truth, the game of life continues anyway, and it will all become clear when we stand before the Umpire of the Universe!

In our folding brochure on the Kingdom of God, we present the question, "What is Kingdom anarchy or insurrection?" To which is given the following answer, "**Kingdom anarchy is: Anyone or anything that fails to cooperate with, or that resists, what the King wants or says, or whom the King sends.**" Please, dear one, *please* don't be so defensive at this point that you miss the point. It's so important that we don't!

Suppose a messenger from Western Union or the Post Office comes to your front door with a message for you. But suppose also that the messenger has something about him that you don't like. Do you reject the message because you don't like the messenger? Many servants of God, and representatives of the King are being rejected daily through people's arrogance and ignorance and independence and jealousy and backbiting and back stabbing and denominationalistic, rutualistic prejudice that has terrifyingly excluded and limited and restrained and restricted and hindered and persecuted Christ Himself, and it **will be** accredited to their account as having been done **to Christ** the way they have treated even the least of those who were doing the will of God!!! **It is accredited to our account (yours and mine) as having been done to Christ, the way you and I relate to the least of His brethren (those who are doing God's will).**

Remember the Kingdom parable of the vineyard where the King goes on a journey, leaving His vineyard in charge of some hireling share cropper tenants? Later He sent His representatives. Remember how angry the evangelical and liberal church leaders of Christ's day became when Jesus told them this parable? This is another ugly example of Kingdom anarchy. (Matt. 21:33-46 . . . Makes interesting reading!) Pray.

"Lord Jesus Christ, Father God, please grant that we never wrongly relate to the Christ in the least of the brethren, (or sisters) and that we may always correctly relate to the Christ **wherever** He is found! We repent, O Lord God, for every and any time that we have failed to correctly relate to You. I receive from You, Father, that godly carefulness lest I fail to rightly relate to Thee.

Dear one, suppose that Christ becomes the Life of the least of the brothers or sisters that are doing the will of God, and you backbite, sow discord and suspicion and division against them. Or fail to feed, clothe, or shelter these who are committed to the will of God? May the Precious Judge of all the Universe have mercy on your soul!!! One would not think of biting off his little finger for an afternoon snack (forgive me this horrible example)—but think nothing of hurting our spouse, family, loved ones, fellow members of the body of Christ . . . (forgive you this horrible sin)!!!

I had a dream in which I was the big white

game hunter with a big game rifle, going through the tall jungle grass, when, to my horror and dismay, I discovered that our quarry, or prey, was a human being. Sure enough, we killed him, cooked him, and I was just ready to take a big bite out of this hairy arm when I awoke. I was nauseated. I said, "Lord, what are You trying to show me?" And it seemed that the Heavenly Father said, "You people in the Body of Christ do **worse** than this, when you sow discord among the brethren in your backbiting and criticism in the Church of Christ Jesus." Then the Scripture came to mind, **"But if ye bite and devour one another, take heed** [take care] **lest you be consumed by one another"** (Gal. 5:15 KJ). May all spiritual vampirism and cannibalism cease from within the Church of the Lord Jesus Christ, and from within your life, and mine—once and for all time, immediately!!! In Jesus' Name, AMEN.

Galatians 5:19-21 gives a list of Kingdom anarchists who "shall not inherit the Kingdom of God." The list is: "Adultery, fornication, . . . idolatry, witchcraft, hatred, variance, [contention], emulations, [jealousy], wrath, strife, seditions, heresies, envyings, murders, drunkenness [alcoholism], revellings and such like: of the which I told you in time past, that they which do [practice] such things shall not inherit the Kingdom of God."

Notice that although alcoholism and immorality are sins we recognize as being "bad" and

"terrible" yet most Christians don't also see the sins of hatred, variance, wrath, strife, seditions, envyings, and such like to be terrible or bad enough to keep (or kick) people out of the Kingdom of God for. I John says that HATRED OF OUR BROTHER IS SPIRITUAL MURDER. One has said that there are more people murdered with the tongue than all the other ways put together.

It is true that practicing alcoholics, fornicators and murderers (saved or unsaved) will be excluded from the Kingdom of God, (unless these dear ones totally and quickly repent), but backbiters, gossips, character assasinators and those who sow discord among the Body of Christ won't make it either! Thus saith the Lord!

In I Corinthians 5:11, God indicates that we are not to keep company, or to eat with, a practicing fornicator or alcoholic if he calls himself a brother, but that list also includes "railers" or those critical of others in the body of Christ. Romans 16:17 says that we are to "mark" and "avoid" those "which cause divisions" in the body of Christ.

But, whether or not we exercise discipline in the body of Christ, nevertheless **it will be accredited to our account, as having been done to Christ, the way we relate to even the least of the citizens of the kingdom of God (those who are doing the will of God!!!)**

Another portion that deals with this same

kind of insurrection is I Corinthians 6:8-10, where
God says, "You yourselves wrong and defraud,
and that your brethren. Or do you not know that
the unrighteous shall not inherit the Kingdom of
God? Do not be deceived; neither fornicators, nor
idolaters, nor adulterers, nor effeminate, nor
homosexuals, nor thieves, nor the covetous, nor
drunkards, nor revilers, nor swindlers, shall
inherit the Kingdom of God."

But, thanks be to God, we don't have to be
rebels to the King, for the very next verse says,
"And such were some of you; but you **were**
washed, but you **were** sanctified, but you **were**
justified in the name of the Lord Jesus Christ and
in the Spirit of our God" (vs. 11). This means,
and the Bible says that these things are forgiveable if a person turns away from these things,
receives God's deliverance and forgiveness and
walks in righteousness.

Christ said that blasphemy of the Holy Spirit
is never forgiveable when they said of Him,
"That's of the devil" (Mark 3). Yet how many
times have you heard Christians glibly say that
about things which may have been of the Holy
Spirit?!!! And why does Jesus say if we call
someone an idiot or a fool we are in danger of hell
fire? (Matt. 5:21, 22). And remember what He
said about causing a little one to stumble (Matt.
18). Pray with me.

Lord of the Universe, we repent of that hideously destructive assassination, cannibalism

and vampirism within the Body of Christ. We see that in order to qualify to be in the Joel's Army of God, that we can't and won't be running one another through. We determine by Your grace before Your face that we shall not be spiritual anarchists. For Thy Kingdom's sake, Amen.

Review Questions

WHEN DID I TOUCH THE KING?

1. Please define "Kingdom Anarchy".
2. Give as many synonyms as you can for Kingdom Anarchy.
3. Give at least 3 (or more) scriptural examples of Kingdom Anarchy.
4. In the parable of the sheep & goats —what was the difference between them?
5. What was the result in each case?
6. What was the same with both groups?
7. Which one will you be?
8. Who are the "least of these" "brothers" "or sisters" of Christ and our brothers or sisters also—that we do it to? (Matt. 12:46-50 and Lk. 8:20, 21)
9. Complete the statement "It is accredited to my account as having been _____ ."
10. What is spiritual vampirism & cannibalism?
11. What is "Blaspheming the Holy Spirit"?

9

WHO'S WHO IN THE KINGDOM OF GOD
or
KINGDOM REVELATION
or
THE GIFT OF SUSPICION

We have a friend named Aleen, who had a friend who was a witch, although Aleen did not know her friend was a witch. This witch would have people pose for a picture instead of signing a guest book. Then the witch would take these pictures and have them dubbed into a compromising photograph so cleverly done that the only way one could tell it wasn't good ol' brother so and so, would be by revelation.

The defeated devil is working increasingly overtime in order to make look good what's bad and to make look bad what's good, so much so that increasingly the only way that we will be able to tell the difference will be by revelation.

That's the only way they were able to recognize Jesus and the disciples in those days, and in these days, too. Please allow for the possibility that had you lived during His time, that you might not have recognzed Him. You might have been one of the religious evangelical leaders of Christ's day plotting His death. It was the liberals, evangelicals and 'fundamentalists' of Christ's day who crucified Him. They read the Scriptures more, fasted more, led more religious lives, kept the legalistic rules. And we can miss Him today also. Yes, you really can!

It's an interesting historical fact that the thing God was doing in one generation has almost always persecuted the thing God did in the next.

The amazing thing about deception is that a deceived person never knows when they are deceived. Thus, we all need to be very humble, taking heed lest we fall. Do you know all there is to know about God? We don't either. So, could we agree to be very patient with one another as we experience this marvelous adventure of being led into all the truth by God's Holy Spirit?

Jesus spoke in parables not to make the message plain, but to make it obscure or hidden from those not entitled to know. "To you it is granted to know the mysteries of the Kingdom of God, but to the rest in parables; in order that seeing they may not see, and hearing they may not understand" Luke 8:10.

And in another place, "At that very time He rejoiced greatly in the Holy Spirit, and said, 'I praise Thee, O Father, Lord of heaven and earth, that Thou didst hide these things from the wise and intelligent and didst reveal them unto babes. Yes, Father, for thus it was well pleasing in Thy sight.' " "All things have been handed over to Me by My Father, and no one knows who the Son is except the Father, and who the Father is except the Son, and anyone to whom the Son wills to reveal Him." "And turning to the disciples, He said privately, 'Blessed are the eyes which see the things you see, for I say to you, that many prophets and kings wished to see the things which you see, and did not see them, and to hear the things which you hear, and did not hear them.' " Luke 10:21-24.

Still another example, "And Jesus answered and said to him, 'Blessed are you, Simon Barjonas, because flesh and blood did not reveal this to you, but My Father who is in heaven.' " Matt. 16:17. This was in response to when "He said to them, 'But who do you say that I am?' And Simon Peter answered and said, 'Thou are the Christ, the Son of the Living God.' " Matt. 16:15,16.

They have perfected the communications media to the extent that they are able to take a number of tapes of a person and from them comprise a thesaurus of words and phrases from which one could manufacture a message, phone conversation, or teaching totally opposite from the original, so that the only way one could tell

who's who or what's what would be by a revelation from God.

THE TRUE BASIS OF LOVE OR A WALK WITH GOD

Contrary to all teaching to the contrary, **the true basis of love, or a walk with God is a commitment of the will based on the will of God!, not on the basis of thoughts, feelings, emotions, imaginations, finances, circumstances or intuitions.**

MOVIEHOUSE OF OUR MIND, OR HINT, HUNCH, AND HUMBUG

Sometimes the enemy is able to sneak into the moviehouse of our mind and portray upon the screen of our conscious awareness lying or invalid or deceptive thoughts, imaginations, feelings, suggestions, emotions, intimations, intuitions, perceptions, convictions, conclusions, assumptions, hints, hunches and humbugs that are not the will of God. But, if you've seen the movie before, or have read the story already, and know how the story is supposed to go, you are o.k. So also, the way to always be sure at the time like that is to switch over to the auto-pilot of the Word of God, the Will of God, and the sure leading of the Spirit of God.

One must never determine the will of God

by looking at feelings, finances, or circumstances, but by the will of God, the Word of God, and the voice of God!

One area where the enemy is able to be most destructive is the marriage. In our book, **The Sexual Ministry**, the topic is discussed at length, but here are a few examples.

THUMPITY THUMP AND FLIP FLOP

On Lover's Lane a week before the marriage, while simply holding hands, the heart was going thumpity thump, the stomach was doing flip flop, there was a zzzt behind the eyes, the knees were weak, the bells were ringing, birds were singing, it smelled like spring time, etc. Now, years later, you come home to your pregnant wife and noisy kids, she's got bad breath, hair in disarray, a pimple on her chin, she's got a cold, no makeup, and for some reason it doesn't smell like spring time and the birds ain't singing. But you love her! Then when you go to the store for some milk, the gal at the checkout register looks like Delilah, Bathsheba, and Cleopatra in one body, and it smells like spring time, and your heart goes thumpity thump and your stomach does flip flop.

For years, Hollywood and Babylon have pushed this lie that love is based on feelings and flip flops, not on a commitment of the will based on the will of God, and that thumpity thumps and spastic thoughts somehow justify adulterous thoughts and acts. If the man at the checkout counter has it together and has not accepted the lie, he can say to Delilah, "God bless you, lady," hand her a Kingdom Gospel Contract, and head on home to the loyal wife of his love. And though, from time to time, the birds don't sing nor bells ring, **nevertheless, the love is sure and strong and pure because that love is based solidly in a firm commitment of one's will, based on the will of God!!!** Everything in our walk with God must have the same foundation. Our worship, praise and rejoicing, our reading of the Word, our attendance and tithing, our love for each other, our being led by the Holy Spirit, must all be based on a choice or commitment of our will, based on the Will and Word of God. Positive emotions will inevitably come. But they must always be the *by-product* of our commitment to do and be the will of God!!! Thus saith the Lord!

REMEMBER: "We wrestle not against flesh and blood, but against principalities, against powers, against the rulers of the darkness of this world, against spiritual wickedness in high places" Eph. 6:12 (KJ).

The following illustrations include several ways in which the defeated enemy tries to bring division and separation and misunderstanding in the body of Christ:

LAUREL & HARDY/ABBOT & COSTELLO

Remember in the cartoons or movies where two friends are walking along when a third person from hiding hits one of the two friends. The hit friend, seeing no one but his friend, assumes that this friend hit him, and says to himself, "I can't let my friend hit me for no good reason." So he hauls off and hits his friend, who says, "I can't let my friend hit me for no good reason." So they are fighting while the enemy is full of glee, still in hiding. It's funny in the cartoons, but not so funny in the family or marriage or in church or among friends.

INVISIBLE WEDGE-SHAPED PRINCIPALITIES

Imagine that the enemy would sometimes send an invisible wedge-shaped principality between you and your friend. If you are not discerning, you may assume that the problem is coming from your friend, and/or your friend from you.

PASS THE TOAST — TWISTER SPIRIT

Imagine a husband and wife sitting at breakfast when the husband says to her, "Pass the toast." But what he really means is, "Darling, I love you so much, I can hardly wait to get home

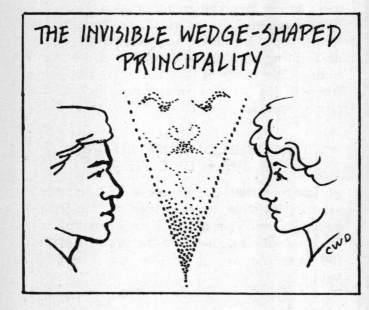

from work to see you, you sweet thing, you are so precious, I'm so glad I married you, and, by the way, would you purty please pass me the toast?" But, remember, all he said was, "Pass the toast." (Maybe he was still waking up.) But suppose she got the wrong impression and that the enemy twisted the intent of his message so that by the time it reached her ears she assumed that he meant, "Hey, you old bag, pass me the toast before I hit you in the mouth." She responds by saying, **"Whaddya mean, 'Pass the toast'? Gidit-cherself."** I've seen this kind of thing happen often in people's interpersonal relationships. But in this illustration, suppose that the husband meant something negative, but because of her love and her trust and her faith, she responded sweetly by saying, "Oh darling, I love you too, you precious sweet thing you, and I can hardly wait to see you, and by the way, here's your toast for my honey." (See our book on **The Sexual Ministry.**) For even though he may have originally meant something negative, he can't help but respond to her faith and trust and love. Get the picture?

HITCHHIKER SPIRIT

We have a friend that people would become aggravated with for no apparent reason. People would want to haul off and hit poor Richard even though he had done nothing to cause this kind of

reaction. Finally, a man of God discerned that the enemy had sent a spirit of aggravation to follow this person to create this kind of reaction in people. Richard was actually a very friendly guy.

IT'S CURTAINS FOR THE ENEMY

Sometimes this situation exists in circles or in waves or curtains around a person especially called of God or chosen of God for a special work or ministry, and usually to the extent of that ministry's importance in the Kingdom of God. In every case, the **Lord has given us power over the enemy, to take authority over the situation.** But in this illustration, when approaching a person, one may feel reactions of rejection, lust, hate, isolation, arrogance, aggravation, confusion, or deception. It is important to **know the person's heart** because these conditions may only exist in the atmosphere around a person who is called of God and who is, in fact, a loving, accepting, humble, anointed man or woman of God. Sometimes, unless a person is very sharp in discerning, one may interpret as coming from another person something that in reality is not in that person's heart, or being.

Remember: **The enemy is always trying to make look bad what's good and to make look good what's bad so that it is always necessary to move in a state of kingdom revelation or discernment.** "Evil men do not understand justice, but **those who seek the Lord understand all things**" Prov. 28:5. Remember— it's the revelation gifts of knowledge, discernment, wisdom—**not** the gift of suspicion! We've known folks and groups who thought of themselves as being spiritually discerning when in fact they were religiously suspicious and doubting.

A man of God has said that he would rather err in trusting love and be wrong by having trusted with faith and love as a basis 999 times, than to be wrong 1 time in 1000 through unrighteous judging, with suspicion and unbelief as its wrong basis.

We've seen churches split, ministries destroyed, restrained, hindered, or delayed, God's glory shamed and the will of God not done because of these things. One cannot describe the unbelievable heartache these things have caused.

One summer when our family was ministering in the eastern half of the country, we heard about a small child that had been attacked and injured by a man. When I heard the details I was almost overwhelmed by a feeling of outrage and righteous indignation. But then the Spirit of the Lord gently reminded me that it's as bad or worse for God's humble children of the Lord to be verbally and spiritually & psychically attacked, abused, dismembered, and murdered by the rest of us in the Body of Christ. On the radio the other day I heard a man preaching from the book of James, that more people have been murdered by the tongue than in all the wars put together in history.

Several scriptures illustrate this:

1) Matthew, Mark and Luke all refer to this one, but we'll quote Jesus in Matt. 18:3-6, " . . . Truly I say to you, unless you are converted and become *like children,* you shall not enter the kingdom of heaven. Whoever then humbles himself *as this child,* he is the greatest in the Kingdom of heaven. And whoever receives one *such child* in My Name receives Me; *But whoever causes one of these little ones who believes in Me to stumble, it is better for him that a heavy millstone be hung around his neck, and that he be drowned in the depth of the sea.*" Here Christ is talking about the humble citizens of the Kingdom.

2) Matt. 5:19-24, "Whosoever therefore shall break one of these least commandments, and shall teach men so, he shall be called the least in the kingdom of heaven: but whosoever shall do and teach them, the same shall be called great in the kingdom of heaven. For I say unto you, That except your righteousness shall exceed the righteousness of the scribes and Pharisees, ye shall in no case enter into the kingdom of heaven.

"Ye have heard that it was said by them of old time, Thou shalt not kill; and whosoever shall kill shall be in danger of the judgment: but I say unto you, That *whosoever is angry with his brother without a cause shall be in danger of the judgment:* and whosoever shall say to his brother, 'Raca,' *[good for nothing]* shall be in *danger of the council:* but *whosoever shall say, 'Thou fool,' shall be in danger of hell fire."*

"Therefore if thou bring thy gift to the altar, and there rememberest that thy brother hath ought against thee; leave there thy gift before the altar, and go thy way; first be reconciled to thy brother, and then come and offer thy gift." (KJ)

3) I John 3:14-18, "We know that we have passed from death unto life, because we love the brethren. He that *loveth not his brother abideth in death.* Whosoever hateth his brother is a murderer: and ye know that no murderer hath eternal life abiding in him. Hereby perceive we the love of God, because He laid down His life for us: and we ought to lay down our lives for the brethren. But whoso hath this world's goods, and seeth his brother have need, and shutteth up his [heart] of compassion from him, how dwelleth the love of God in him? My little children, let us not love in word, neither in tongue; but in deed and in truth." (KJ)

I John 4:20-21, "If a man say, I love God, and hateth his brother, he is a liar: for he that loveth not his brother whom he hath seen, how can he love God whom he hath not seen? And this commandment have we from Him, That he who loveth God love his brother also." (KJ)

It is right to be outraged at the Atlanta murderer, or the Nazi slaughters, but we need to feel *equal or greater* outrage at the spiritual, psychic, emotional, or mental murders and assaults and torments WE members of the body of Christ commit against each other as husbands, wives, brothers, sisters, family members, pastors, evangelists, members of the body of Christ—and especially the 'humble ones' who are trying earnestly to fulfill the will of God and the Great Commission—the brothers and sisters and mothers of Christ. When Paul was persecuting *the Christians* Jesus said, "Why are you persecuting ME? (Acts 9:4b), and, "I am Jesus whom you are persecuting" (vs. 5).

GOD'S WISDOM VS. MAN'S

Please study with me for a moment about the nature of this revelation knowledge and wisdom and how it works from this scripture:

"That your faith should *not rest on the wisdom of men,* but on the power of God. Yet we do speak wisdom among those who are mature; a wisdom, however, *not of this age,* not of the rulers of this age, who are passing away;

"But we speak *God's wisdom* in a mystery, the hidden wisdom, which God predestined before the ages to our glory;

"The wisdom which none of the rulers of this age has understood; for if they had understood it, they would not have crucified the Lord of glory;

"But just as it is written, 'Things which eye has not seen and ear has not heard, and which have entered the heart of man, all that God has prepared for those who love Him.'

"For to us God revealed them through the Spirit; for the Spirit searches all things, even the depths of God.

"For who among men knows the thoughts of a man except the spirit of the man which is in him? Even so the thoughts of God no one knows except the Spirit of God.

"Now we have received, not the spirit of the world, but the Spirit who is from God that we might know the things freely given to us by God,

"Which things we also speak, not in words taught by human wisdom, but in those taught by the Spirit (of God); combining *spiritual thoughts* with *spiritual words*.

"But a natural man does not accept the things of the Spirit of God; for they are foolishness to him, and he cannot understand them, because they are spiritually appraised.

"BUT HE WHO IS SPIRITUAL (not unspiritual) APPRAISES ALL THINGS, YET HE HIMSELF IS APPRAISED BY NO MAN.

"For who has known the mind of the Lord that he should instruct Him? But we have the mind of Christ" I Cor. 2:5-16.

Job's friends were *wrong*. Eli the priest was *wrong* with Samuel's mother. David's brothers were *wrong* when he wanted to kill Goliath. Saul was *wrong* when he wanted to kill Jonathan. And you may be wrong also! Remember: **the greatest key to knowing the will of God is to have a deep Deep DEEP commitment to DO THE WILL OF GOD!!!** (John 7:17)

I say again, do you know all there is to know about God? We don't either. But can we agree to be patient with each other in this marvelous adventure of being led into all truth by the Holy Spirit?

MOST DISLIKED BIBLE VERSE

I have a least favorite scripture. Remember that verse where Jesus, after walking with the disciples for three years, told them, "I have many more things to say to you, but you cannot bear them now" John 16:12? I don't want the Lord to have to say that to me. Remember that definition of the RUT: a shallow grave without any end? God, deliver us from our ruts, and from every negative conditioning of our thinking, every limitation on our expectancy, every barrier to overflowing faith!!! And cause us to be a people that You can lead into all truth, revealing that which is to come, revealing to us the things of Christ. In Jesus' Name, Amen.

This, then, is the means by which we recognize the citizens and messages and representatives of the Kingdom of God. **A representative of the Kingdom of God is ANYONE THE KING HAS CHOSEN TO REPRESENT HIM IN**

ANY REGARD, and who is FUNCTIONING UNDER Christ's Lordship and Love.

"I praise Thee, O Father, Lord of heaven and earth, that Thou didst hide these things from the wise and intelligent, and didst reveal them to babes" Luke 10:21.

In the last two chapters, we have been talking about the importance of unity in the Body of Christ, and now about knowing the will of God. Here is something that ties these two thoughts together:

BODY GUIDANCE

There should be more allowance in the Body of Christ for each other to be led sovereignly by God, led by the Holy Spirit. Romans 8:14: "For as many as are led by the Spirit of God, they are the sons of God" (KJ). Sometimes God leads in strange ways and it behooves us not to be critical of the way God may be sovereignly leading. Acts 21:14 gives an example of a difference of opinion, that was only solved by the dear ones in lovingly committing this brother to the grace of God and saying, "The will of the Lord be done!" Instead, sometimes we will purposely, psychically intimidate and alienate our brother or sister when we think they are not doing the will of God as we see it for them. But this is not fair or wise. We can tell them what we think, but *then* it is our responsibility *not* to judge or be critical. Their

God, Jesus Christ, has a right to lead them, without obtaining *your* approval. In that case, we lovingly commend them to the grace of God and love them and pray for them and keep the door open to them. If they are wrong, they will have difficulty enough, now or later, without us adding to their problem our judgment and criticism. Jesus is still saying to us today, "What is that to thee? Follow thou Me!" (John 21:22b)

Recently, I became freshly impressed that it is not enough for me to accept Christ as my Lord alone, but it is also necessary for me to accept and receive Christ Jesus as The Lord of my brother and sister in Christ . . . as your Lord too!!

God be merciful to all of us as we seek diligently to please Him in everything.

Romans 14 is good in this regard. Now we are NOT talking about things in the Bible that God has clearly said is sin. But there are a multitude of other areas where we are guilty of judging. Verse 4, "Who art thou that judgest another man's servant? to his own master he standeth or falleth . . . " (KJ)

So, we see that there is such a deep need for us to love each other unconditionally, without criticism or walls, or character assassination or resentment. The Lord says that it is not enough to love one another *tolerantly,* but that we are to "obey the truth through the Spirit unto *unfeigned* love of the brethren, see that ye **love one**

another *with a pure heart fervently!!!*" (I Pet. 1:22) Now Please Pray with me.

We worship You, Oh Lord of the Universe, Lord Jesus Christ, and we also will be careful to honor You and appreciate You in our brother and in our sister! We repent for not having rightly related to You in the least of the brothers and sisters. And ask that by Your grace we will always rightly relate to You wherever You are found.

We ask You, Lord Jesus, for the Spirit of Wisdom, Revelation and the Knowledge of our God to rest upon us, unceasingly—increasingly. Yea, Lord, Be our Life. Love through us with a pure and fervent practical 'I Corinthians 13' and 'I John' type of love. In Jesus Christ's Name we pray and believe, Amen.

Review Questions

THE GIFT OF SUSPICION

1. Complete this sentence. The defeated devil is working overtime trying to make look good _____ _____ and to make look bad _____ _____.

2. How will we know the difference?

3. What groups responsible for crucifying Christ, compare with today? (Not Jews)

4. What is the only way the disciples were able to recognize Christ? Then—now?

5. T or F: That which God did yesterday has almost always persecuted what God is doing today.

6. Yes or No: Do you know all there is to know about God?

7. T or F: A deceived person never knows when he is deceived.

8. T or F: Jesus spoke in parables to make the message plain.

9. Complete this sentence: The true basis of love or a walk with God is _____ .

10. Name at least 5 things that are totally unreliable indications of the will of God.

11. Name at least 2 things that are always reliable indications of the will of God.

12. Complete this Kingdom principle: "One must never determine the will of God by looking at a) _____ , b) _____ , c) _____ , but by d) _____ ,

e) _____, f) _____.

13. Name at least 5 symptoms of "being in love" that are not at all valid in determining whether or not one is loving according to the will and Word of God.

14. If a person "falls out of love" with one's spouse and "falls in love" with someone else—does this justify adulterous thoughts and/or actions?

15. Explain as briefly as possible the following illustrations on disunity:
    a) Laurel & Hardy
    b) Invisible Wedge-Shaped Principalities
    c) Pass the Toast
    d) Hitchhiker
    e) Curtains for the enemy.

16. What sins in the body of Christ are equal to, or worse than a child murderer or the Nazi criminals?

17. On the basis of John 7:17, what is the best way to know the will of God?

18. What was the definition given of a "rut"?

19. Define "Kingdom Representative".

20. In addition to receiving Christ as OUR Lord, what is also necessary in our attitude toward our brother/sister in Christ?

21. What is meant by the phrase "psychic intimidation"?

22. What does Rom. 14:4 say?

23. How does I Peter 1:22 say we are to love each other?
    a) _____, b) _____.

10

ABC'S OF KINGDOM
INITIATIVE—OUTLINE

I. Most people expect God to do what God expects people to do!
   a. Psalm 149
   b. Psalm 2
   c. "Whatsoever ye bind . . . shall be bound . . . Matt. 18:18 (KJ).
   d. "Whatsoever ye loose . . . shall be loosed . . ." Matt. 18:18 (KJ).
   e. "Shall God not also speedily avenge His own elect which cry day and night unto Him?" Luke 18:7.
   f. "If two of you shall agree on earth as touching anything that they shall ask, it **shall be done**" Matt. 18:19 (KJ).
   g. "Ask and ye shall receive" Matt. 7:7, 8.
   h. "Seek and ye shall find" Matt. 7:7, 8.
   i. "Knock and it shall be opened unto you" Matt. 7:7, 8.
   j. " . . . Until now the Kingdom of Heaven

suffers violence, and violent men [or people of intense zeal of the Lord] take it by force" Matt. 11:12.

k. "The weapons of our warfare are not carnal, but are mighty through God to the pulling down of strongholds" II Cor. 10:4.

l. "And this Gospel of the Kingdom shall be preached in all the world for a witness unto all nations; and **then** shall the end come" Matt. 24:14 (KJ).

m. "Go ye into all the world, make disciples of all nations, teaching them to **do all** that I have commanded you" Matt. 28:18-20 (JB).

n. "Go out into the highways and hedges, and compel them to come in, that My house may be filled" Luke 14:23 (KJ).

o. "Do the work of an evangelist . . . be instant in season, out of season" II Tim. 4:2, 5 (KJ).

p. "Pray ye therefore the Lord of the harvest, that He will send forth labourers" Matt. 9:38 (KJ).

q. " . . . Pray ye that your flight be not in the winter, neither on the Sabbath day" Matt. 24:20 (KJ).

r. "Go ye into all the world, and preach the Gospel [of the Kingdom of God] to every creature" Matt. 16:15 (KJ).

s. "Whosoever shall call upon the Name of the Lord will be saved" Rom. 10:13-15.

t. "[God is] not willing that any should perish" II Pet. 3:9 (KJ).

u. "If you see your brother hungry and feed him not . . . " James 2:15-20 (JB).

v. "Humble yourselves . . . " I Pet. 5:6 (KJ).

w. " . . . Work the works . . . the night cometh" John 9:4 (KJ).

x. "The one who endures to the end . . . will be saved" Matt. 24:13.

y. "Wherefore criest thou unto me? Speak . . . that they go forward" Ex. 14:15 (KJ).

z. "Love one another . . . " I Pet. 1:22; I John 3:23; etc.

II. God will *not* do sovereignly what He has commissioned **US** to do in His sovereignty through **US**!!! But thanks be to Him, God's commands are God's enablements. Literally, every command God makes speaks to our initiative.

A through Z above: After each point ask the question, "What will happen if **WE** don't do our part of the promises/commands? (Ans.: Either it will not get done, or God will raise up someone else through whom to do it!, or maybe finally we will do what we should!)

IT'S YOUR MOVE
or
KINGDOM INTIATIVE
or
IF GOD WILLS IT, WILL IT HAPPEN???

I was in a situation the other day where I wanted to make a good impression. Perhaps the whole city would open up to the ministry if I had made a good impression. It was the state capital and a large city. I wanted to make a good impression and to keep the good impression I had made. But I had to call a man of God on a destructive statement he had made. Very destructive, and yet, the whole crowd seemed to agree with him. Friend, let me tell you something. **You can not be a man-pleaser and remain in the Kingdom of God. The fear of man brings a snare on every level and in every place. Spiritual prostitution is the worst prostitution of all. It is that which compromises to gain, keep, or curry favor.** *If a man has a sell-out price, satan will come up with the silver.*

I saw a political cartoon the other day in which a politician was posing for a picture, but was inadvertently standing beside a "for sale" sign. It reminded me of so many "would-be" but won't-be men of God—as long as they are for sale.

The destructive statement this gentleman made was: "Well, if God wills it, it will happen," and, "We'll be able to tell if it is the will of God by whether or not it happens."

Please let me explain why I believe this fatalistic thinking and acting, (or should we say lack of action) is so destructive! Look at the following Scriptural examples:

1. "Ask and it shall be given you; seek and ye shall find; knock and it shall be opened . . ." Matt. 7:7-8 (KJ). Question: What will happen if we do **not** ask, and seek, or knock?

2. "Whosoever shall call upon the Name of the Lord will be saved" Rom. 10:13-15 (KJ). Question: What will happen to those who do not call? "[God is] not willing that any should perish" II Pet. 3:9 (KJ). Does that mean everyone will be saved? no, No, **No!**

3. "And how shall they hear without a preacher?" I've heard folks say of some ministries, **"If God is in it, it will go."** But the Word says, **"How shall the preacher preach except he be sent?"** Rom. 10:13-15 (KJ). Sometimes we are at each other's mercy!

4. What would happen if the 'Godly ones' in Ps. 149 did not exercise their privileges and did **not** "bind [the] kings with chains?" **not** "execute vengeance upon the heathen?" **not** "execute pun-

ishments upon the people? and not "execute upon them the judgment written?"

5. Jesus said, "From the days of John the Baptist until the present time, the Kingdom of Heaven has endured violent assault, and violent men seize it by force . . . the most ardent zeal and intense exertion" Matt. 11:12 (AMP). Question: Will the Kingdom be taken if men and women of the white hot zeal of the fiery intensity of the Lord of the Armies of the Universe don't take it???

6. Jesus said, "He that shall endure unto the end, the same shall be saved" Matt. 24:13 (KJ). Question: What happens if we don't endure to the end???

7. In the next verse Jesus says something very important, (doesn't He always?) He says, **"And this gospel of the Kingdom shall be preached in all the world for a witness unto all nations; and then shall the end come!!!"** Matt. 24:14 (KJ). Question: Will the end come before this Gospel of the Kingdom is preached in all the world??? Come on, you lazy laggard, I curse to hell your insipidity, lethargy, passivity, and bondage! I prophesy the Mighty Lion of the Tribe of Judah to rise up within you and that you rise up from the dust, oh daughter of Zion, and shake yourself like a lion going forth to take a prey!!!!

8. Jesus said, "Whatsoever ye shall bind . . . . shall be bound, and whatsoever ye shall loose, shall be loosed . . . !!!" Matt. 18:18 (KJ).

But what if we don't bind??? And what if we don't loose??? Sweet, sweet sister of the Saviour, and my precious brother in the Lord, **If you don't bind, it won't be bound; and if you don't loose, it won't be loosed!!!** unless our Sweet and Precious Saviour someday, somewhere, somehow, sometime raises up someone to do what you were supposed to have done!!! The only problem is that **"The night is coming when no man can work!"** So we had better **"Work the works of Him [that sends us] as long as it is [yet] day!!!"** (John 9:4) Will you help us? We are willing to help you. That's only one reason why we wrote this book.

9. Jesus said, "Shall not God [also speedily] avenge His own elect, which cry day and night unto Him . . . ?" Luke 18:7 (KJ). But what happens if we don't cry day and night unto Him? Will we be speedily avenged of our adversary?

10. "Work out your own salvation with fear and trembling" Ph. 2:12 (KJ). What if we don't?

Tell, me, precious theologian, what will happen if we don't use "the weapons of our warfare [that] are . . . mighty through God to the pulling down of strong holds?" II Cor. 10:4 (KJ). [That's a big "10:4"]. What will happen if we don't "go into all the world" and obey the Great Commission? What if we don't "compel them to come in?" (Luke 14:23) If we don't "do the work of an evangelist?" If we don't "pray the Lord of the harvest to send forth laborers?" (Matt. 9:38) If we don't pray that our flight won't be on the Sabbath or in winter time? (Matt. 24:20)

Thus saith the Lord, If we don't do it, either it won't get done, and Christ's return will be delayed, or He'll have to raise up someone else to do it, or maybe, just **maybe, you will finally get with His program**!!! Let's just hope to God it will be in time! How many of the dear ones have gone to hell because you and I haven't told them? How many sick are dead, or still suffering because of **our** passivity and disobedience? How many marriages have broken up because WE didn't share a better way with them? How many people have been murdered, mobbed, or mugged, maimed, or massacred because you and I didn't do **our** part in binding and loosing?

You may be objecting to this harassment, saying that I am trying to put you under condemnation. Dear one, are you willing for some good old-fashioned **conviction**??? I pray God Himself to mess with you and me, and mess with us until we are smack dab in the middle of the sweet, sweet, perfect will of God!!! Thus saith the Lord, "From this day forth, we are free to do the will of God. We are free to be led by the Holy Spirit." In Jesus' Name, Amen.

Please look at this! If you have received Christ **as your life** and believe that He is living His Life in you, and that you are seated on His throne in Him with the Father, and that He is living in you and that He *has* blessed you with

Every thing in Him, then won't the Christ in you be exercising some aggressive initiative? Won't the zeal of the Lord of Hosts be demonstrated through you?

Over and over I hear people advise, prophesy, or pray, "Don't strive", "Don't be 'out of rest' ", "Don't 'lean on the arm of flesh' ". If I were satan, I would try to get people to be passive, and that's exactly what he's done! But **God** says, "Woe to those who are at ease in Zion!" (Amos 6:1)."Cursed be he that keepeth back his sword from blood." (Jeremiah 48:10b) Imagine telling Christ to not be "out of rest", etc., when He was sweating great drops of blood in the garden, or when He was driving the money changers out of the temple, or when He was seeking the Father's face with strong crying and tears!!! Right doctrine is False doctrine when wrongly applied, and the Church of Jesus Christ needs to **wake up!!!** **We prophesy to the sleeping giant of the church of Jesus Christ to wake up!!!**

Then the man of whom I spoke at the beginning earlier advised me, "Don't lean of the arm of flesh." I told him, "Mister, I'll tell you what's of the flesh—laziness, passivity, lack of love, apathy, lethargy, insipidity, lassitude, lack of obedience. Fiddle faddling while the world burns, or letting people go to hell forever, and live in hell in the meantime, **is of the flesh**, if we could have rescued them."

The people that say, "Don't strive", should

read scriptures like:

1. Luke 13:24, "Strive to enter in at the straight gate." (KJ)
2. Rom. 15:30, "Strive . . . with me in your prayers. (KJ)
3. Rom. 15:20, "So have I strived to preach." (KJ)
4. Phil. 1:27, "With one mind, striving . . . for the faith." (KJ)
5. Col. 1:29, "Striving according to His working." (KJ)
6. Heb. 12:4, "Ye have not yet resisted unto blood, striving against sin." (KJ).

Jesus said, "And from the days of John the Baptist until the present time the kingdom of heaven has endured violent assault, and violent men seize it by force [as a precious prize]—a share in the heavenly kingdom is sought for with the most ardent zeal and intense exertion" Matt. 11:12 (AMP).

Oh how the Christ within us wants to accomplish His works in the earth! But there exists a real problem in the Church! You see, we have been passively **waiting for God to do what He has been waiting for us to do**—have been asking Him to do what He's told **us** to do. But **now the time has come** when God's people shall respond to the call of God! The prophecy of Isaiah 59:16-19 comes true, "Rise up oh Daughter of Zion from the dust; shake thyself and wrap thyself with zeal as a cloak; go forth with the spirit of the Mighty Lion of the tribe of Judah, to take a prey, to see God's Kingdom come, God's will be done on earth as it is in heaven. Having clothed thyself with the razor sharp, white hot, fiery zeal of the Lord of the Armies of the Universe. For 'from the days of John the Baptist until now the Kingdom of Heaven suffers violence', but now comes forth those of 'the most ardent zeal and intense exertion' of the Spirit of the Lord to Make it Happen!!!"

Picture Christ Himself living within you, wanting, waiting to do what He wants to do in and through you, while you are praying to a long-distance-God-in-heaven to do sovereignly for you what He already waits to do in and through you! Remember that scripture, "But the righteousness based on faith speaks thus, 'Do not say in your heart, "who will ascend into heaven?" (that is to bring Christ down), or "who will descend into the abyss?" ' (that is, to bring Christ up from the dead). But what does it say? 'The **word** [rhema] is near you, in your mouth and in your heart' " Rom. 10:6-8. Jesus is the **Word**—He is in you as your Life! Amen.

Remember what we said about Christ Himself being our Life? Well, **this is the short cut** to the fulfillment of the Will of God!: "You are not sufficient of yourself so as to think anything of yourself, but **your sufficiency is of God, who**

makes you an able minister of the cove-
nant!!!'' (II Cor. 3:5, 6 KJ).

These next truths will help you put wings and
wheels on the fulfillment of the will of God in
your life!!! Pray this prayer, now.

Dear Heavenly Father, In Jesus' Name we
come to You. We come boldly, humbly into Your
Throne Room to stay forever, and to find help in
this time of need. We deeply repent of the dead
works that clutter our lives, and we intensely
pursue the Leading of the Lamb of God **wherever**. We would be those Spirit led sons of God.
We volunteer to be your Joels' Army soldiers of
the Lord, who hear Your voice and do Your will
now and forevermore, Amen.

We reckon the old life to be completely dead,
and embrace You as our Life. We embrace Your
discipline as our discipline, and by Thy grace
shall do those Living Works and speak those
creative words. We believe Thee, receive Thee to
be now all You are, in us!!! Now and forevermore, Amen.

Review Questions

DO IT NOW!

1. What is the worst kind of prostitution?
2. Complete the saying,"If a man has a sell-out price _____ _____ _____ ____ _____ _____ _____."
3. If God wills something, will it happen?
4. What will happen if we do not knock, seek, or ask?
5. Is it true that if God is "in" a ministry, will it go? Explain:
6. Who are the "godly ones" or "the saints" spoken of in Ps. 149?
7. Describe what is meant by violence in its 2 usages in Matt. 11:12.
8. Matt. 24:13. What will happen if we don't endure to the end?
9. Matt. 24:14. Will the end come if the Gospel of the Kingdom is not preached in all the world?
10. What if we don't bind or loose?
11. Can we guarantee that God will speedily avenge us of our adversary if we don't cry day and night unto Him?
12. T or F: There is a kind of striving in the Bible that is good.

13. Complete this sentence: We have been waiting for God to do what He has been _____ .

14. What does II Corinthians 3:5, 6 say? "Not that we are sufficient _____ ."

11

WHAT'S SO EASY ABOUT WALKING WITH GOD?!
or
KINGDOM DISCIPLINE
or
IT'S GOTTA BE EASIER THAN THIS?

One day Wells asked me, "John, how do you discipline yourself to read the Word and pray?" And upon doing a quick introspect, discovered that in spite of former struggles with discipline and failure in discipline, that now, I was, in fact, spending much precious time in prayer and in the Word—but without the previous struggle. I was surprised with myself that I was breezing along in a high level of "discipline" but without discipline's ugly struggle!!! My answer to Wells was, "It does not seem to be a discipline, but is a matter Life or death, and my seeking the Lord and His Word seems to have become as automatic and important as breathing."

Our oldest son, Joseph, had problems with asthma. It was so terribly frustrating to watch Joey fight for each breath of air, while breathing for the rest of us was no problem. I believe that one is spiritually less than healthy if we have left our first love, are undisciplined, unloving or lukewarm, where spiritual breathing becomes a labor or discipline or when spiritual hunger is lacking.

The biggest problem with discipline is that most people are **disciplining the wrong thing!!***
Most people apply discipline to the old life, the old nature, the sin nature, the old self, the black dog nature, the carnal nature . . . but this is gross futility because they are applying discipline to the very thing that Christ took with Him to the cross. And Christ killed it, crucified it, and buried it!!! Remember, Christ brought you forth from the grave a whole, new, beautiful, adequate, sufficient, glorious, wonderful, superior, divine Creation—fashioned in God's image—that Jesus Christ **is the life of.** And He is also the discipline of that divine creation. If Christ Jesus is your Life, you'll be disciplined, because Jesus is disciplined. He got up a great while before day to pray, fasted often, sought the Father's face with strong crying and tears, prayed through the night sometimes, left the crowds to pray, learned obedience through the things He suffered, always did the things that pleased the Father. And you will also, if Christ is your Life!!! Because Christ

---

*The discipline of a dead corpse.

was the most disciplined One of all, and He still is!!! The best way to get wrinkles out of a gunny sack is to fill it with the golden grain. "This I say then, walk in the Spirit, and ye shall not fulfill the lust of flesh" Gal. 5:16 (KJ).

So, the thing you and we are to focus on is not the discipline of a dead corpse, for you have died, and your Life is hidden with Christ in God!!! (Col. 3:3). Thanks be unto **"Christ, who is our life!!!!"** For as You, Lord, are revealed, we also are revealed gloriously with You. **Allelujahweh!!!!!!!!!!**

By the way, this **LIFE** is not yours without appropriation on your part, for you are to **reckon yourself to be dead indeed unto sin, but alive to God in Christ Jesus**. (Rom. 6:11)

One of our friends, Polly Christopher, asked me one time, "John, it seems that in order to walk with the Lord, you've got to be a spiritual masochist,* or at least it would help." After thinking a minute I replied, "No, Polly, I believe in order to walk with God, really close, it would help if one were a **'SANCTIFIED HEDONIST'** "! I went on to explain, "Polly, if I were suddenly to swap, scrap, or trade all of my present scruples, moral ethics and Kingdom Principles in exchange for a new principle or philosophy of selfishness in which I decided that I was going to do what was best for me, what advantaged me, the most pleasure for me, the highest high, greatest 'kicks', longest 'trips'—that **I WOULDN'T**

---

* A glutton for punishment.

CHANGE A THING—Not one thing!"

Remember when we talked about this? There is a discipline that we embrace, but that discipline pertains entirely to the New man, the new nature, the new Life in Christ! In the same way that Christ embraced discipline for His sinless life, and as Adam *should* have embraced discipline in order Not to sin, we may also be *privileged* to embrace the discipline of Christ. We are to discipline our new life as Christ did His—because He **is** our New Life!

Hebrews, in chapter 5 talks of this regarding the life of Christ (Remember, He did no sin, had no "sin nature".)

> "Who in the days of His flesh [He had flesh], when He had offered up prayers and supplications with strong crying and tears unto Him that was able to save Him from death, and was heard in that He feared; Though He were a Son, Yet learned He obedience by the things which He suffered; And being made perfect, He became the Author of eternal salvation unto all them that obey Him" (vs. 7-9 KJ)

If Christ is our Life, living in us, we will be as Jesus was in this passage. Jesus went through this process to demonstrate to us that WE CAN DO IT TOO. "I can do all things through Christ" Phil. 4:13 (KJ).

Let me ask you a question. Have you accepted Jesus as your Lord? In Matt. 7:21, Jesus makes it clear; "Not every one that saith unto

Me, 'Lord', 'Lord', shall enter into the Kingdom of Heaven; but He that doeth the will of my Father which is in heaven." (KJ)

For example, there are many who claim and talk about the fact that Jesus is their Lord, but in fact are not doing His will, for one of the following excuses:

1. Don't know what His will is.
2. Too busy 'making a living'.
3. Don't know His voice well enough.
4. Don't know His Word well enough.
5. Don't have enough time.
6. Not holy enough.
7. Not smart enough, educated enough.
8. Not strong enough, old or young enough.
9. Not enough faith.
10. Not the right time, too soon, too late.
11. God didn't "call" them.

Tell me, for you'll have to tell the Lord Jesus at the Judgment Seat of Christ, *what's your excuse for not doing the Father's will?* But make no mistake, there is no acceptable excuse under heaven for not doing the will of God. The only substitute for the will of God is the will of God!!!

But so often I hear people say, "But it is too hard to walk with God and serve and obey Him in this way of discipleship." Please consider these three scriptures:

1. "The way of transgressors is **HARD**" Pr. 13:15b (KJ)

2. " . . . it is **HARD** for thee to kick against the [ox goad]" Acts 9:5b (KJ)

3. "Come unto Me, all ye that labour and are heavy laden, and I will give you rest. Take My yoke upon you, and learn of Me; for I am meek and lowly in heart: and ye shall find rest unto your souls. For **MY YOKE IS EASY!!!** and **MY BURDEN IS LIGHT!!!**" Matt. 11:28-29 (KJ).

We ask you again, "What will you trade for your walk with God?" For six years as a probation officer for Los Angeles County, I saw people who were being paid the "wages of sin". Do you want the devil for a master? No thanks. I'm just not interested in hangovers, guilt feelings, venereal disease, or an eternity in hell! (Forever is a long, long time to burn!!!!!)

This whole thing about the Lordship and reign of Jesus Christ can be boiled down to one question, **"WHO IS SMARTER, YOU OR GOD?"** For if God loves you (and He does), and if the Lord Jesus Christ has your best interest in mind (and He does), then you should let Him run your life. But if you are smarter, then you should decide your own career, who you're going to marry, where you will live, how to spend your time and money, not God. But if God is smarter, then to that same extent, we should insist that He be the Lord and King over our life, our family, our business, church, home, property, possessions, finances, future, eternal destiny, and everything-Everything-EVERYTHING!!!

Jesus said, "What will a man give in exchange for his own soul?" Eve traded hers for an apple. Adam traded his for Eve. Satan traded his for hell. Esau traded his for some bean soup. What will you trade for yours????? I said, what will you trade for your soul? Jesus said, "What will it profit a man if he gain the whole world, but lose his own soul in hell" Matt. 16:26 (JB). **FOREVER IS A LONG, LONG TIME TO BURN!!!!!!!!** As for me and my friends, we chose the following:

1. "Joy unspeakable and full of glory" I Pet. 1:8 (KJ)
2. "The abundant Life" John 10:10 (JB)
3. "Fullness of joy" John 15:11, Ps. 16:11 (KJ)
4. "Pleasures forever more" Ps. 16:11 (KJ)
5. "All things richly to enjoy" I Tim. 6:17 (KJ)
6. "Every spiritual blessing" Eph. 1:3 (KJ)
7. "Always more than a conqueror" Rom. 8:37 (JB)
8. "All my needs supplied" Phil. 4:19 (JB)
9. "Uttermost parts of the earth for [my] possession" Ps. 2:8 (KJ)

And infinitely more!!! God said, "Eye hath not seen, nor ear heard, nor has it entered anyone's heart, the fantastic things that God has prepared for those of us who love Him!!!" I Cor. 2:9 (JB)

Perhaps you are asking, "What will all this cost me?" The answer is, "It will cost you everything you have and are in exhange for everything God has and is."

The story is told of a wealthy but discontented old gentleman who was riding on a train observing the serene smile and radiant countenance of a Salvation Army lassie. He spoke to her, "Miss, I would give everything to have your radiant smile and your peaceful countenance." To which she replied, "That is exactly what it would cost you, Everything."

Another story is told of a little girl whose most valued possession was a dirty string full of pretty, but peeling, plastic play pearls. One day her father came to her and said, "Darling, would you be willing to give to your father your pretty, but peeling, pile of plastic pearls? I would like for you to give them to me as a gift." She said, "But what would my father want with some old pearls? Daddy, I really love them!" But finally she gave them to him, whereupon he just threw them into the fire on the hearth, where they were destroyed. Then the father drew from his pocket a lovely golden chain, upon which were strung the most precious and beautiful genuine pearls in all the world, which he gave to the now totally contented girl. Your Heavenly Father is asking you to give Him your life which, for the most part, has amounted to just a dirty old string of petty, peeling, pitiful, plastic play pearls by comparison to the Abundant Life He has for you!!! Please pray this prayer.

Dear Lord God of the Universe, I now give to Thee my whole life, my future, my family, my business, my sins, my resentment, my bitterness, my futility, my everything, my right to myself in exchange for my right to unlimited access to You, Your Life, Your peace, Your wealth, Your joy, Your Saviour, Jesus Christ, Your salvation, Life and discipline, Your perfection. I give You everything I have and shall ever have. Lord God and Heavenly Father, Precious Lord Jesus, I believe that You are smarter than me, and that You have my best interest in mind. Therefore I now, and shall always, give away all that I am and shall ever be, to You, dear God of gods, King of kings and Lord of lords, Lord Jesus Christ. Amen.

Lord, by Your grace, grant me always the sweet leading of Your Holy Spirit and that I shall never cast away my "confidence which has great recompense of reward, because afterward, I shall receive what is Promised." I choose in advance to pay whatever price is necessary to be the kind of Overcomer that shall rule the world with You. Therefore, the "sufferings of this present time are not worthy to be compared with the Glory which shall be revealed in [and to and from and around] us. ALLELUJAHWEH! ! ! Rom. 8:18 (KJ)

---

*Hebrews 10:35-38 (JB)

Review Questions

WHAT'S SO EASY ABOUT WALKING WITH GOD?!

1. What's perhaps the biggest problem or misconception about discipline?
2. List several (at least 7) qualities or adjectives that describe the new you that Christ brought forth from the grave.
3. What's the best way to get wrinkles out of a gunny sack?
4. Name at least four things about the life of Christ that indicate His discipline of Himself which will also be true in you if Christ is your life?
5. According to Galatians 5:16, what's the best way to NOT walk in the flesh?
6. What is meant by the phrase "sanctified hedonist"?
7. Describe the prayer life of Jesus in the days of His flesh in Hebrews 5:7-9.
8. Name at least five of the main excuses people give for not doing the will of God?
9. What has your main excuse been for not doing the will of God?
10. Will any of these excuses be good enough at the Judgment Seat of Christ for not doing the will of God?
11. Which is easier—to serve God or satan?

(Explain if you like)

12. Who is smarter, you or God?

13. When are you demonstrating that you think that you are smarter?

14. What would you trade for your soul? What's your sell-out price?

15. How much does it cost to be in the Kingdom of God? How much are the membership dues?

16. Make a list of at least 20 things you have given, now give and shall always give, to the Lord 100%.

17. Make a list of at least 20 things you get from God as a gift.

18. Please complete this scripture: Hebrews 10:35, 36, "Cast not away your confidence _____ ."

12

HOW MUCH DOES IT COST?
or
"PENNY" COST

Rom. 8:18—"I reckon that the sufferings of this present time are not worthy to be compared with the **glory that is to be revealed in us**."

Acts 14:22—"Strengthening the souls of the disciples, encouraging them to continue in the faith and saying 'Through many tribulations we must enter the Kingdom of God.' "

Rom. 8:17—"And if children, heirs also, heirs of God and **fellow heirs with Christ** if indeed we suffer with Him in order that we may also be glorified with Him."

Why do so many "converts" to Christianity convert to something else when trouble comes? The missionary term for this is "Rice Christians" or those who are faithful as long as there is rice being handed to them.

As we have said, we say again, Christianity's greatest need is discipleship, motivated by love,

Matt. 28:18-20. We need teaching that produces loving disciples, or those who give up **all** for love of the Lord Jesus Christ.

There are many of the dear ones who are neither willing to leave, nor give of, their prosperity to see the Great Commission fulfilled. That's why it hasn't been fulfilled.

Like the rich Christian businessman who after giving his testimony of how God made him rich after he gave his "seed" money investment gifts, a little old lady stood in the back and said, "I dare you to do it again!" (Are you smiling??)

Many times people have said to those who are committed to do the will of God and the fulfillment of the Great Commission, "Be warmed, be blessed, and be fed, but I'll be blamed if I'll give you my stuff" James 2. On the basis of Matt. 25, some of them will be blamed because they didn't.

So also will be those who did not endure until the end. (Matt. 10:22) The invitation of Christ is still "Come and suffer with Me." I challenge you to get a complete concordance and look up all the verses on suffering and tribulation. Do you want the Kingdom of Heaven? Then remember Jesus' words, "Blessed are those who have been persecuted for the sake of righteousness, for theirs is the Kingdom of Heaven." Matt. 5:10.

WHAT SUFFERING?

One needn't look for it, for it shall be the inevitable by-product to those who are committed to the will of God. The will of God runs cross current to the will of the world, the will of our friends and will of our flesh.

Many pray yes with Paul (Ph. 3:10) "Oh to know the power of His resurrection" (JB), but then say no to the "fellowship of His sufferings."

The invitation of Christ and the challenge of the Great Commission is still the same—"Come and suffer with us."

"Woe to them that are at ease in Zion" Amos 6:1 (KJ).

The Christ who said, "Those who are not against Me are for Me" (Mark 9:40 JB), also said, "Those who are not for Me are against Me" Matt. 12:30 (JB). Sometimes when you set your face like a flint to do the will of God, your foes will become "they of your own household", or "the household of faith".

Christ praised Peter, but a few verses later said to the rock on which at least one church was supposedly built, "Get behind Me Satan" (Matt. 16:23 JB), when Peter became a distraction. And that must be our loving but firm attitude as well, with those who would distract or hinder us from the will of God!

There are those who are willing to leave all but the good graces and the good opinions of their spouse, family, friends and dear ones. Whose opinions and good graces are you willing to leave all but????

I know old David never saw the righteous begging bread, (Ps. 37:25) but the Son of Man had no place to lay His head (Matt. 8:20). And sometimes neither will you if you follow Christ (Heb. 11:37, 40).

I know Paul said, "My God shall supply all my need" Phil. 4:13, but also said, "We are afflicted . . . perplexed . . . persecuted . . . struck down . . . constantly being delivered over to death for Jesus' sake" . . . "much endurance, in afflictions, in hardships, in distresses, in beatings, in imprisonments, in tumults, in labors, in sleeplessness, in hunger, in dishonor, by evil report . . . unknown . . . dying . . . pushed . . . sorrowful . . . poor . . . having nothing . . ." II Cor. 4:8, 6:4. I challenge you dear ones: "Except a man give up **all he has**, he cannot be My disciple" Luke 14:26-33 (JB). The scripture that says "What ever we ask, we receive of Him . . ." is preceded five verses earlier by, "But whoever has the world's goods, and beholds his brother in need and closes his heart against him, how does the love of God abide in him?" I John 3:14-24. I was proud that the parable of the man with the bigger barns didn't apply to me since I didn't want God to say, "Thou fool—this night thy soul shall be required of thee!!" Then I saw the application where Jesus said, "So is he that layeth up treasure for himself and who is not rich towards God."

We believe in prosperity. But we believe that

the purpose of prosperity is the fulfillment of the Great Commission!!! We are personally aware of many who are prepared and ready to preach the gospel, teach, evangelize and suffer for Christ, with no provision; but surrounded by people who only have enough money for things that are higher on their priority list than God's priorities. No, I'm not against prosperity, but I'm in favor of discipleship, saving people from hell and helping people receive Jesus Christ. Are you willing to suffer for Christ enough to wait on God long enough to know His voice and do only His will for your life? There can't be anything more important than this. Don't you agree? Remember you gave your time, your self, your all to Him. Now watch the marvelous adventure unfold as you are committed to be the disciplined unrestricted channel of His Glory.!!!

You don't have to buy a burlap bag to wear under your underwear. All you have to do is do the will of God. If you do you'll suffer. But if you suffer with Christ, you'll reign with Christ, and this "momentary light affliction is producing for us an eternal weight of glory far beyond all comparison!" II Cor. 4:17. For "all that will live Godly in Christ Jesus shall suffer persecution" II Tim. 3:12 (KJ). But the "Sufferings of this present time are not worthy to be compared with the glory which shall be revealed in us" Rom. 8:18 (KJ.)

The joy that comes from doing God's will, far

surpasses and obliterates the pain of our sacrifice for Christ. And our sacrifice so great is so small compared to the Love of God and the Joy set before us—Only play pearls or pennies by comparison! If we suffer with Christ, **we'll reign with Him!!!!** Do you think it was a sacrifice for the man to sell all he had, to buy the field with the hidden treasure in it? The treasure was able to buy infinitely more than he had before!!!

Remember: The cost is everything we have and are and will ever have and be in exchange for all that God has and is.—Let's pray!

Lord Jesus, God of all things, I pay the price. I give my all to Thee. But I can already see that I'm getting the best of the exchange! Thank You, Lord, Amen.

God is looking for a qualified people into whose hands He can commit unlimited glory, wealth, power and authority. Are you willing to qualify?

Review Questions

HOW MUCH DOES IT COST? "PENNY" OR COST?

1. What is a "Rice Christian"?
2. According to Matthew 25, why did the goats go to hell?
3. Is it really necessary for a disciple to suffer?
4. What is absolutely necessary for a person to give up in order to be Christ's disciple according to Luke 14:26-33?
5. What's the main purpose of God given prosperity?
6. Fill in the missing word. In order to reign with Christ, it is necessary that we_____with Him.

Chris Wold Dyrud

13

POWER OF PERSUASION
or
THE TERROR OF THE LORD
or
KINGDOM EVANGELISM

Perhaps some of you are saying, "Where do we go from here?" The answer is, of course, **"Go ye into all the world and make disciples of all nations, teaching them to obey everything I have commanded you . . . "** coupled with the command and promise, **"Seek ye first the kingdom of God and His righteousness** and all these things will be added unto you!" The promise with the Great Commission is twofold: **"All authority has been given to Me in heaven and on earth"** and **"Lo, I am with you always even unto the end of the age".**

One of the first things of necessity is to know the **voice of the Lord.** Jesus said, "My sheep hear My voice," (John 10:27) and Rom. 8:14 says, "For all who are being led by the Spirit of

177

God, these are the sons of God." **Question**: Suppose you are going down a certain path and the Holy Spirit tells you to turn right, but you insist on going straight, either because you did not hear the Lord or were disobedient after hearing. Are you then in the will of God? Are you under the Lordship of Christ in the Kingdom of God or are you acting anarchistically? **The Kingdom of God is what God is the King of**, or the Lord over. Here is an interesting fact to consider: "If God is not being allowed to be your Lord, then He's not being allowed to be your Lord."

Jesus said, "I always do those things that please the Father!" John 8:29. Paul said, "The blood of no man is on my hands. I've been faithful to the heavenly vision." "I've fought a good fight, I've finished my course, henceforth is laid up for me a crown of righteousness that no one can take" (Acts 26:19; 20:26; II Tim. 4:5-8). And we can be able to say these things, too!

THE VOICE OF THE LORD

I am so impressed with the incredible way God talked to our sisters and brothers in both the Old and New Testament!! It is amazing to me how these dear ones had a "name and address" knowledge of the voice of the Lord. And this one thing marks the greatest difference between evangelism as we have known it and what we call "Kingdom Evangelism", for Kingdom Evangelism is directed by the King!!! For example God spoke to the parents of John the Baptist about his name and life, and also to Mary and Joseph about Christ—to the wise men and shepherds, to Paul about Macedonia, and the shipwreck, to Ananias about Paul on the street called Straight, and inquired at the house of Judas for one called Saul. God spoke to Moses, Noah, and John about measurements and specifics. And God wants to speak specific things to us as well. While Elijah was hearing God's voice tell of the ravens, the brook and the widows—his fellow prophets were hiding and starving in caves. When the Father spoke from heaven to Christ in an audible voice—some standing by thought it thundered. (John 12:21-50). What did it sound like this morning when God specifically spoke to you?

Many times people will say—"God told me this" or "thus saith the Lord" when God did not saith. Often people will say "my witness is . . ." when they should say "my opinion is" . . . while passing off their hunch as the infallible word of God Almighty.

There is an unnecessary famine for hearing the voice of the Lord. Unnecessary—because God wants to speak specifically to you if you will care to dare to listen and respond.

JESUS SHOWED US HOW!

Jesus taught us how to know the Father's

voice. Here let me quote two verses of Jesus regarding His own "modus operandi" or mode of operation, which to Him was a way of life. From the Amplified New Testament, John 5:19, "So Jesus answered them by saying, I assure you, most solemnly I tell you, the Son is able to do nothing from Himself—of His own accord; but He is able to do only what He sees the Father doing. For whatever the Father does is what the Son does in the same way [in His turn]" and now John 5:30, "I am able to do nothing from Myself —independently, of My own accord; but as I am taught by God and as I get His orders. [I decide as I am bidden to decide. As the voice comes to Me, so I give a decision.] Even as I hear, I judge and My judgment is right (just, righteous), because I do not seek or consult My own will—I have no desire to do what is pleasing to Myself, My own aim, My own purpose—but only the will and pleasure of the Father who sent Me."

Aren't these amazing? But let me point out something which I believe shall make so much difference! If Jesus operated this way, and felt that He, **God**-man that He was, could do nothing from Himself—then it seems that weak us should all the more have this as our way of life also!!!

There is that place of voluntary utter hopelessness and helplessness apart from the Lord Jesus and the Heavenly Father, even though we are omnipotent in Him!!! But a sad fact is that almost no one knows God's voice in this way!!!

Jeff asked me why this is so. I believe it is because we haven't seen either the possibility or the importance of knowing the voice of the Lord in this way! But we are trying to avoid the futility of an entire life of misdirected effort and wasted time!

So also in evangelism directed by the King. Suppose that you decided to adopt a new plan of action for your life in which you determined not to do or say anything unless and until you were first by the Lord shown and told to do and say that thing? How your life would change! But think about it! Think of how your friends would misunderstand; of how you would immediately begin seeking the Lord as you perhaps never have before!!! Think of how you would be forced to learn God's voice. Think of how productive your life would suddenly become and of how at last your efforts at evangelism and every other endeavor would suddenly blossom into a level of fruitfulness never before dreamed possible. If Jesus, for example, would have healed Lazarus from being sick instead of raising him from the dead, He would have missed the bull's-eye of the will of God and committed the sin of "hamartano", or missing the mark.

HOW DO YOU LEARN GOD'S VOICE?

1. Be His sheep, be born again. "My sheep hear My voice," said Jesus in John 10:27.

2. Be totally committed to God's will regardless—John 7:17, "If any man is willing to **do His will**, he shall know of the teaching [leading] whether it is from God . . . " (J.B.).

3. Be totally free from sin—I John 1:9, because sin's condemnation makes it difficult for one to hear God's voice.

4. But the biggest reason folks don't know God's voice is because they haven't seen the need nor have they had the burden. The price to be paid is the price Christ paid in Hebrews 5:7, 8, 11-14, "In the days of His flesh [Jesus] offered up definite, special petitions [for that which He not only wanted but needed], and supplications, with strong crying and tears, to Him Who was [always] able to save Him (out) from death, and He was heard because of His reverence toward God—His godly fear, His piety [that is, in that He shrank from the horrors of separation from the bright presence of the Father].

"Although He was a Son, He learned [active, special] obedience through what He suffered.

"Concerning this we have much to say which is hard to explain, since you have become dull in your [spiritual] hearing and sluggish, even slothful [in achieving spiritual insight].

"For even though by this time you ought to be teaching others, you actually need some one to teach you over again the very first principles of God's Word. You have come to need milk, not solid food.

"For every one who continues to feed on milk is obviously inexperienced and unskilled in the doctrine of righteousness, [that is, of conformity to the divine will in purpose, thought and action,] for he is a mere infant—not able to talk yet!

"But solid food is for full-grown men, for those whose senses and mental faculties are trained by practice to discriminate and distinguish between what is morally good and noble and what is evil and contrary either to divine or human law" (AMP).

What a marvelous adventure to live like Jesus did in that He always only spoke what He heard the Father speaking. Even in churches that teach a "Spirit led" walk with God, too often there is a protracted infancy because of over dependence on the spiritual leaders for guidance. Also, as long as someone else is making the decisions, you take little or no responsibility for your actions and decisions. But God's mature sons are those who know God's voice and follow the leading of the Holy Spirit. And He is looking for the sons that will deny enough selfish expenditure of time to learn His voice on a level deeper than hint, hunch and humbug. These Holy Spirit directed activities will make for dynamic and effective evangelism like Philip directed by the Holy Spirit in the book of Acts.

HOW TO DO KINGDOM EVANGELISM

The first step, of course, is to be born again; (John 3:3, 5) then to be totally yielded to Christ 100%. (Rom. 12:1, 2) Also, be full to overflowing with the Anointing of God, the Holy Spirit. Also, have no sin, having been cleansed from all unrighteousness. (I John 1:9) Then, **with the leading of the Holy Spirit,** make it happen! It helps if one has a pamphlet that's really good. We have an excellent brochure available for distribution entitled, "Kingdom Contract", especially designed for this purpose.

How To Do Kingdom Evangelism: (The following guidelines will be helpful)

A. Spiritual Guidelines:
1. Know Christ Jesus as your own personal Saviour, by inviting Him in to take over completely, as Saviour, Lord and Life!
2. Be totally yielded and dedicated to Christ 100%.
3. Be filled to overflowing with the Spirit of God and His anointing.
4. Be cleansed from all unrighteousness, (I John 1:9) having no sin.
5. Have a right spirit, with no resentment, bitterness, or unforgiveness.
6. Be alive with the Fruits of the Spirit; Love, etc.

7. Go forth in the Authority of the Lord with Christ as your Life, being seated in the Heavenly places, with Christ Himself fulfilling His Evangelistic ministry through you, speaking His words through you, working His miracles and works through you, moving through you in the gifts of the Holy Spirit, discernment, faith, wisdom, knowledge, etc.

B. Other Suggestions:

1. It is IMPORTANT to have READ YOUR BIBLE THROUGH AT LEAST ONCE in your Christian Life. If we took a survey of 10,000 average born again Christians, I believe that less than 1% would be able to say that they had read the entire Bible at least once. In other words, I would be surprised if more than 1 out of 100 could say they had at one time or another read every verse in the Bible at least once. The reason this is so important is that the Holy Spirit is able to bring everything to our remembrance that He has taught us, or that we have read in the Word of God. Jesus promised us that. If a carnal scientist can enable us to recall everything that we have experienced with our senses, under hypnosis or the electronic or chemical stimulus of the brain, then how much more on a supernatural level can the Holy Spirit bring out of our

mental and spiritual computer all the Scriptural and spiritual things we have programmed into it!! But you can see that if we have not read the Word, we can not expect, except by a special miracle, God to bring to our remembrance things we never were exposed to in the Word in the first place. Comes out of the computer, only what has been programmed into it! (a) So we suggest that you begin today with Matthew chapter 1, and (b) after completing each chapter—*write the day's date after that chapter*, and then (c) hurry on to the next. As soon as you have completed the New Testament, then hurry (d) thru the Old Testament. (e) Don't worry about understanding. Things that seem boring or unclear have constant light shed upon them in your later praying and reading. (f) Don't skip any parts. What an Adventure!!

2. Another practical suggestion is to have some literature along, telling how to be born again and walk with God. Make sure that there is given the phone number or address of one whom they can contact as they need more help. Also make sure the literature deals with Christ as Master, Boss and Lord. Many tracts do not. If you would like copies of our "Kingdom Contract" brochure, contact

us. It has the contents of this book summarized in a few words. (Also available in Portuguese.)

3. Obtain, if possible, their address and phone number (for follow-up).

4. As soon as possible, sometimes even before anything informational is exchanged, ask them to pray responsively as you lead them in prayer. For example, one day while working at the Christian Broadcasting Network, (CBN), at Love Lines, a caller called up and by the end of his first sentence, I could tell his spiritual state of needing to be born again. So, before he even completed his first sentence in the problem, I interrupted and asked him if he would allow me to lead him in prayer, with him following responsively. Before we were into the conversation only 3½ minutes, he had accepted Christ as his Saviour, Lord and Life, and had received the Holy Spirit and was asking for more information to be sent to him. There are times when the Holy Spirit will direct in this way! So many Scriptural examples of this underscore the point: Think of all the many times Christ would walk up to someone—out of the blue— and say, **"follow Me"**. And do you know what? They followed Him! And there are literally multitudes who are

waiting for someone to tell them where to go, what to do, which way to go, what to believe. You who smuggly sit back in your easy chair and criticize the cults, **you and I are to blame!** People wouldn't be eating that garbage if we were out there feeding them something more tasty! But if we don't tell them, **"how shall they hear?"** However if we get people born-again, but not discipled to Christ as absolute Master, then we still have not fulfilled the Great Commission! **"Go ye into all the world, make disciples,"** not just get them "born again", but make mature disciples who will do anything God tells them. Matt 28:18-20.

5. Bind the strong man; (Matt 12:29) take authority over the blindness, and loose to them the spirit of repentance, speak them into a place of deliverance and life. Thus more and more people are coming to appreciate and exercise the use of: THE POWER OF THE SPOKEN WORD.

THE KINGDOM CALL
or
THE PLAN OF SALVATION IN TWO WORDS

ELIJAH AND ELISHA
" . . . and Elijah passed by him, and **cast his**

mantle upon him. And he left the oxen, and ran after Elijah, and said, Let me, I pray thee, kiss my father and my mother and then I will follow thee. And he said unto him, Go back again for what have I done to thee? And he returned back from him, and took a yoke of oxen, and slew them, and boiled their flesh with the instruments of the oxen and gave unto the people, and they did eat. Then he arose, and went after Elijah and ministered unto him" I Kings 19:19-21. (KJ)

JOHNATHAN AND THE ARMOR BEARER

I Sam. 14 (whole chapter) "Let's go and make it happen!" (JB) And they did.

CHRIST AND MATTHEW

"[Jesus said], '**Follow Me**.' And he [Matthew] arose and followed Him" Matt. 9:9 (KJ).

CHRIST AND PETER AND ANDREW

"[Jesus said], '**Follow Me**, and I will make you fishers of men.' And they straightway [immediately] left their nets, and followed Him." Matt. 4:19-20 (KJ).

CHRIST AND JAMES AND JOHN

"**He called them**. And they immediately left the ship and their father, and followed Him." Matt. 4:21-22 (KJ).

CHRIST AND THE DEAD BURIER

" 'Lord, suffer me first to go and bury my

father.' But Jesus said unto him, "**Follow Me**, and let the dead bury their dead' " Matt. 8:21-22; Luke 9:60 (KJ).

CHRIST AND THE RICH YOUNG RULER

"Jesus said unto him, 'If thou wilt be perfect, go and sell that thou hast and give to the poor and thou shalt have treasure in heaven: and **come and follow Me**' " Matt. 19:21, Mark 10:21 (KJ). How about you? Would you like to be perfect? Most of us would have gotten this person "saved" in no time at all and had him elected to the deacon board. That's another difference between Kingdom Evangelism and evangelism.

CHRIST AND ANYONE

Jesus said to His disciples, "If any man will come after me, let him deny himself, and take up his cross and **follow Me**" Matt. 16:24, Mark 8:34 (KJ). Jesus is calling you, too.

CHRIST AND PHILIP

He found Philip, and Jesus said to him, "**Follow Me**" John 1:43 (KJ).

THE MASTER AND THE SLAVE

And the master said to the slave, "Go out into the highways and hedges and **compel them to come in**, that My house may be filled" Luke 14:23 (KJ).

CHRIST AND THE GREAT COMMISSION

"Go therefore and **make disciples** of all the

nations, baptizing them in the name of the Father and the Son and the Holy Spirit, teaching them to observe all that I commanded you . . . " (It's not enough to get people "saved".) Matt. 28:19-20; Mark 16:15 (KJ).

PAUL AND HIS FOLLOWERS
"Be ye followers of me, even as I also am of Christ" I Cor. 11:1. (See also I Cor. 4:16 and Ph. 3:17) (KJ) Can we say this to people?

TO WHOM DOES THE GREAT COMMISSION APPLY?

To whom does the Great Commission apply? For those of you who are not sure what the Great Commission is, we are referring to Christ's commission that He gave in Matt. 28:18-19. "And Jesus came up and spoke to them, saying, '**all power (authority) is given to Me in heaven and on earth. Go therefore and make disciples of all the nations, baptizing them in the name of the Father and the Son and the Holy Spirit, teaching them to [obey] all [everything] that I commanded you; and lo, I am with you always, even unto the end of the [world].' "**

So we ask the question: "To whom does this Great Commission apply?" Theoretically, the commission was given to the eleven disciples. But **notice**: Jesus said, "Teach them (**everyone**) to obey **everything I have commanded** you!'' And, of course, we see that one of the most important things Christ commanded them was the Great Commission which the disciples were to teach us that we are also to obey!!! Do you see this? The Great Commission then applies to us every bit as much the same as to the early disciples.

RELATED SCRIPTURES

"And sent His servant at supper time to say to them that were bidden, **'come; for all things are ready'** " Luke 14:17 (KJ).

" . . . The Master of the house **being angry** said to His servant, **'go out quickly** into the streets and lanes of the city, and bring in hither the poor, and the maimed and the halt and the blind' " Luke 14:21 (KJ). God is saying this now, also.

"And the Lord said unto the servant, 'Go out into the highways and hedges and **compel them to come in,** that My house may be full' "!!! Luke 14:23 (KJ). The Lord is saying this now!

THE JUDGMENT SEAT OF CHRIST

"For we must **all appear before the judgment seat of Christ;** that every one may receive the things done in his body, according to that he hath done, whether it be good or bad. **Knowing therefore the terror of the Lord,** we persuade men . . . " II Cor. 5:10.

I. **A FACT**

   "For we must all appear before the judgment seat of Christ; that everyone may receive the things done in his body, according to that he hath done, whether it be good or bad" II Cor. 6:10 and verse 11a (KJ).

II. **A MOTIVATION—"Knowing therefore the terror of the Lord, we persuade men . . . "**

   A. Daniel 12:2-3—"And many of them that sleep in the dust of the eath shall awake, some to everlasting life, and some to shame, and everlasting contempt. And they that be wise shall shine as the brightness of the firmament; and they that turn many to righteousness, as the stars for ever and ever." (KJ)

   B. JUDE 14-15—"And Enoch also, the seventh from Adam, prophesied of these, saying, 'Behold, the Lord cometh with ten thousands of His saints. To execute judgment upon all, and to convince all that are ungodly among them of all their ungodly deeds which they have ungodly committed, and of all their hard speeches which ungodly sinners have spoken against Him.' " (KJ)

   C. Rev. 20:12—"And I saw the dead, small and great, stand before God; and the books were opened; and another book was opened, which is the book of life; and

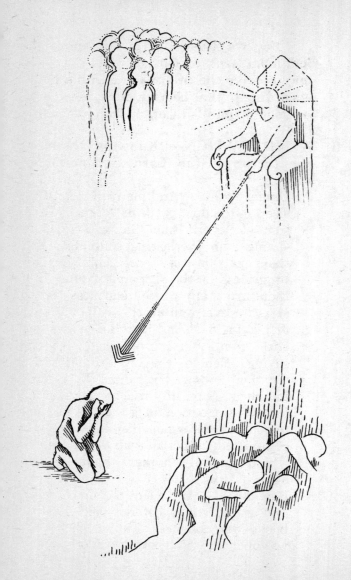

the dead were judged out of those things which were written in the books, according to their works." And verse 13, "And the sea gave up the dead which were in it; and death and hell delivered up the dead which were in them; and they were judged every man according to their works." (KJ)

D. Eccl. 12:14—"For God shall bring every work into judgment, with every secret thing, whether it be good, or it be evil."

E. I Cor. 3:12-15—"Now if any man build upon this foundation gold, silver, precious stones, wood, hay, stubble;

"Every man's work shall be revealed by fire; and the fire shall try every man's work of what sort it is.

"If any man's work abide which he hath built thereupon he shall receive a reward.

"If any man's work shall be burned, he shall suffer loss: but he himself shall be saved; yet so as by fire." (KJ).

F. Heb. 10:31—"It is a fearful thing to fall into the hands of the living God!" (KJ)

III. AN INEVITABILITY

A. Matt. 13:41-42—"The Son of Man shall send forth His [messengers], and they shall gather out of His Kingdom all things that offend, and them which do iniquity; And shall cast them into a furnace of fire: there shall be wailing and gnashing of teeth." (KJ)

B. JOHN 15:6—"If a man abide not in Me, he is cast forth as a branch, and is withered; and men gather them, and cast them into the fire, and they are burned." (KJ)

IV. A SURPRISE

A. The Five Foolish Virgins—Matt. 25
1. They were virgins.
2. They had lamps.
3. They were waiting.
4. They said, "Lord, Lord."
5. The door was shut.
6. Jesus said, "I know you not."

B. The Sheep and the Goats—Matt. 25
1. Both groups said, "Lord, when did we treat You like this?" (JB)
2. To both groups Jesus answered, "When you did it to the least of My brothers, (or those who are doing God's will)!" (JB)
3. Both groups were clean animals.
4. Both groups were eternally rewarded (Sheep/Kingdom—Goats/Fire & Punishment)

C. The One Talent Man—Matt. 25
1. He had a talent.
2. He had a relationship with the

Master. (He was a bond slave.)

3. He had a commission.
4. He had maintained what he had been given, and gave it back to God.
5. His talent was taken away.
6. He was called a wicked and slothful person. (Was made to feel shame)
7. He was cast into outer darkness.
8. He was exiled to a place of weeping and teeth gnashing.

D. The Sons of the Kingdom. "But the children of the Kingdom shall be cast into outer darkness: there shall be weeping and gnashing of teeth." Matt. 8:12 (KJ).

V. A PUNISHMENT
   or
VI. A REWARD
VII. WHO SHALL BE SAVED

A. Matt. 19:29—"And everyone that hath forsaken houses, or brethren, or sisters, or fathers, or mothers, or wife, or children, or lands, for **My** Name's sake, shall receive an hundredfold [10,000%] and **shall inherit everlasting life**." (Luke 18:29 says "For the Kingdom of God's sake.")

B. GALATIANS 6:8—"For he that soweth to his flesh shall of the flesh reap corruption: but *he that soweth to the Spirit* shall reap life everlasting."

C. Matt. 24:13—"But *he that shall endure*

unto the end, the same shall be saved." (KJ)

D. I JOHN 2:3, 17—"And hereby we do know that we know Him, if we keep His commandments . . . And the world passeth away, and the lust thereof: but *he that doeth the will of God* abideth forever." (KJ)

E. I JOHN 3:6-10—"Whosoever *abideth in Him* sinneth not; whosoever sinneth hath not see Him, neither known Him. Little children, let no man deceive you: he that doeth righteousness is righteous, even as He is righteous. His seed remaineth in him: and he cannot sin, because he is born of God. In this the children of God are manifest, and the children of the devil: whosoever doeth not righteousness is not of God, neither he that loveth not his brother." (KJ)

F. I JOHN 5:18—"We know that whosoever is born of God sinneth not; but he that is begotten of God keepeth himself, and that wicked one toucheth him not." (KJ)

G. MARK 16:15-18—"And He said unto them, 'Go ye into all the world, and preach the Gospel to every creature. He that believeth and is baptized shall be saved; but he that believeth not shall be damned. And these signs shall follow them that believe; **in My name** shall they cast out devils; they shall speak with new tongues . . . they shall lay hands on the sick and they shall recover."

H. JOHN 3:16—"For God so loved the world, that He gave His only begotten Son, that *whosoever believeth in Him* should not perish, but have everlasting life."

I. Rom. 10:9 (Whole chapter)—"That if thou shalt *confess with thy mouth* the *Lord Jesus,* and shalt *believe in thine heart that God* hath raised Him from the dead, thou shalt be saved." (KJ)

J. Rom. 8:13—"For if ye live after the flesh, ye shall die: but if *ye through the Spirit do mortify the deeds of the body,* ye shall live. For as many as are led by the Spirit of God, they are the sons of God." (KJ)

K. Heb. 3:14—"For we are made partakers of Christ, *if we hold the beginning of our confidence steadfast unto the end."* (KJ)

L. Heb. 10:26-27—"For if we sin willfully after that we have received the knowledge of the truth, there remaineth no more sacrifice for sins. But a certain fearful looking for of judgment and fiery indignation, which shall devour the adversaries." (KJ)

M. Heb. 10:38-39—"Now the just shall live by faith: but if any man draw back, My Soul shall have no pleasure in him. **But we** are not of them who draw back unto perdition; but of them to the saving of the soul." (KJ)

LOST YOUR SALVATION?

I would like to say just a word here to those who wonder if they may have "lost" their salvation by sinning too badly. If pious platitudes or counsel doesen't work or if you can't receive assurance by any other means—let me encourage you. We see on the basis of Ephesians 2:8-10 that none of us *deserve*, or could earn, salvation. It is a gift. In other words—none of us could ever hope to *earn* or deserve salvation. Therefore—none of us deserves more than an eternity in hell—much less anything better. We don't deserve to be treated fairly, we don't deserve life, liberty or pursuit of happiness. Any thing good we get above hell—is God's gracious undeserved giving—even a rainy day, a cup of chlorinated water, a blade of grass. We don't *deserve* anything good. In other words if you served God perfectly for 70 years—He would still be just in keeping you out of heaven, because you can't *earn* heaven. You don't deserve heaven. But you can receive God's free gift! But you don't "earn" a gift by working for it. You simply receive it and enjoy it. That's how to be born again. Simply receive gratefully God's Son Jesus Christ to be all that He is—in you as your total Lord and Life and Salvation. And then express your gratitude by Living happily ever after in Him, for Him!

But if you feel that God Has rejected you

according to Hebrews chapter 10, here's what I propose: You already know what you deserve. But what does the King deserve? Christ deserves your loyalty, your praise, your service, your righteous living and acting, your giving, your prayers and fellowship, your reading of the Word, your helping of God's people, etc. So never mind what you deserve. That's God's business. Just concentrate on giving Christ what He deserves. That's your business!

KINGDOM EVANGELISM

I. JESUS IS THE EVANGELIST — (the Spirit's operation)
    A. "The Spirit of the Lord is upon Me, because He hath anointed Me to preach the Gospel to the poor; He hath sent Me to heal the brokenhearted, to preach deliverance to the captives, and recovering of sight to the blind, to set at liberty them that are bruised, To preach the acceptable year of the Lord." Luke 4:18 (KJ). (He as our life will be fulfilling His ministry through us!)
    B. "I came not to call the righteous but sinners to repentance" Luke 5:32 (KJ).
    C. "For the Son of Man is not come to destroy men's lives, but to save them. And they went to another village" Luke 9:56 (JB).

II. JESUS IN US IS THE EVANGELIST (by our Appropriation)

A. Gal. 2:20—"I [have been] crucified with Christ: nevertheless I live; yet not I, but Christ liveth in me: and the life which I now live in the flesh I live by the faith of the Son of God, Who loved me, and gave Himself for me." (KJ)

B. Col. 3:3-4—"For ye are dead and your life is hid with Christ in God. When Christ, Who is our Life, shall appear, then ye shall also appear with Him in glory" (KJ). Why wait?!

C. Ph. 4:13—"I can do all things through Christ [Who] strengtheneth me." (KJ)

D. Ph. 1:21—"For me to live is Christ, and to die is gain" (KJ).

E. Ph. 2:13—"For it is God which worketh in you both to will and to Do of His good pleasure" (KJ). Also Rom. 12:1; Rev. 3:20; Acts 1:8; John 5:30

III. JESUS EVANGELIZES—(Through our co-operation) MOTIVATION
   A. OBEDIENCE
      1. The Great Commission—Matt 28:18-20 (read)
      2. The Great Compelling—Luke 14:23 —"And the Lord said unto the servant, 'Go out into the highways and hedges, and **compel them to come in,** that My house may be filled!" (KJ)
   B. LOVE—John 14:15—"If ye love Me,

keep My commandments." (KJ)

1. The Great Commandment—"Jesus said unto him, 'Thou shalt love the Lord thy God with all thy heart, and with all thy soul and with all thy mind' " Matt. 22:37 (KJ).

2. The Great Commandment—"And the second is like unto it, 'Thou shalt love thy neighbor as thyself.' " Matt. 5:43 (KJ); 19:19; 22:39; Mark 12:31; Luke 10:27; Rom. 13:9; Gal. 5:14; Ja. 2:8, etc.

ETERNALLY SECURE?

There are many, many people who have prayed the "sinner's prayer" and have "accepted Christ" that are counting on a false sense of security who will be hideously dissappointed at the Judgment seat of Christ.

And there are many ministers who will be horror stricken at the false sense of security they imparted. Juan Carlos Ortiz in his book *Disciple* talks of the Greasy Grace "Fifth Gospel of the Saint Evangelicals" that has nothing to do with the Gospel of the Kingdom. We recommend that book. Of course we must be born again. But there's more to life—and the Great Commission—than being born.

In the physical realm there are those special

people who are physically, emotionally or mentally undeveloped past infancy though they may be 40 years old. And our churches are full of special 40 year old spiritual infants who haven't graduated from nursery school. They don't know God's voice, don't wait on God, don't read God's Word, don't know God's Word, don't spiritually reproduce. Thus saith the Lord! If we don't make obedient disciples of these—and of dear ones throughout the earth—then we haven't fulfilled the Great Commission.

Furthermore, it is both heresy and false doctrine to assure people that they will inherit heaven by calling Christ "Lord" if they don't also *do the will of* the Lord. Our salvation is not a thing or a doctrine but a Person—His name is Jesus Christ. Let us abide in Him. God's gracious gift of Himself!

Pray with me, please.

Lord Jesus—Our Sweet and Strong Salvation. We hear Thy voice calling us to abide in Thee. We also respond to Your commission to bring forth spiritual children—**tall strong sons and daughters of God.** You said that when we follow You—You make us fishers of Men. Thank You Lord—Amen.

Review Questions

POWER OF PERSUASION

1. Where do we go from here?
2. What are the promises given in Matthew 6:33 and in Matthew 28:18-20?
3. According to Romans 8:14, what is the main proof of whether or not a person is a "son of God"?
4. If you are going down the street and the Holy Spirit tells you to turn right and you don't because you don't hear or care—are you in the will of God? Is God being your King in that specific thing? Have you sinned?
5. What is meant by "name and address" leading of the Lord?
6. What's the main difference between evangelism and Kingdom evangelism?
7. What does John 5:19 & 30 say as to Christ's modus operandi (the way He operated or did things)?
8. What should our mode or method of operation be?
9. What is "hamartano"?
10. What is meant by "hint, hunch or humbug" leading?
11. What is the single most important ingredient to knowing God's voice that people will do almost anything but?
12. List some of the main causes of "protracted

infancy" in the body in Christ.

13. Give a brief but complete set of instructions how to tell people to read the Bible through.

14. Give Christ's plan of salvation in two words.

15. To whom does the Great Commission apply? Why?

16. Who will stand before the Great Judge of all the Universe?

17. What two things will we be held responsible for?

18. What 5 things will happen to those of us who do not continue to abide in Christ according to John 15:6?

19. Name 4 positive things about the foolish virgins in Mt. 25.

20. What 2 negative things happened?

21. Why did the goats go to hell? (Mt. 25)

22. Name four positive things about the one talent man. (Mt. 25)

23. What four things happened to him.?

24. How did people get eternal life in the following passages? Matt. 19:29; Mark 10:29; Luke 18:28-30.

25. According to Matt. 14:13, who shall be saved?

26. According to Gal. 6:8, how does one reap life everlasting?

27. According to I John 2:3, what is the proof of knowing God?

28. According to I John 2:17, who shall abide forever?

29. Quote I John 5:18.
30. According to Heb. 3:14, how are we made partakers of Christ?
31. According to Heb. 10:26-27, what will happen to us if we willfully sin after we have received the knowledge of the truth?
32. What should we do if we think we have "lost" our salvation?
33. Who is the only effective evangelist?

Chris Wold Byrud

14

KINGDOM RESOURCES AND OPPORTUNITIES
or
What About Money?

If a bank, finance company or lending institution offered to give their investors a 20%, 30% or 100% return on their money, they would be flooded with business! Yet the Lord Jesus Christ offers you more than this! Jesus guarantees to you in writing that if you invest your money in the Kingdom of God, you will gain more than a 30% return on your investment; more than 70%; more than 200%; more than 1000%; but an incredible 10,000% return on your investment of money or any valuable commodity!!! No lie—a 10,000% return on your investment! In fact, Jesus prefaced His promise of 10,000% return on your investment in writing by saying, "Verily I say unto thee" or "I assure you, most solemnly I tell you", or "I especially promise!"

Here is the whole written guarantee in God's

own Words: "And Jesus answered and said, "Verily I say unto you, there is no man that hath left house, or brethren, or sisters, or father, or mother, or wife, or children, or lands, for My sake, and the Kingdom of God, and the gospel's, but he shall receive an **hundredfold** [One hundred times as much, or 10,000%], **now in this time**, houses, and brethren, and sisters, and mothers, and children, and lands, with persecutions; and in the world to come eternal life" Mark 10:29-30 (KJ), and Luke 18:28-30 and Matt. 19:29.

Do you understand how this works? If the banker or savings and loan officer says to you, "If you give me your money, I'll give you back 20%, what he means is "I'll give you back $1.20 for every dollar you give to me." 100% return would be $2.00. 1000% would be $10.00. 10,000% return on your investment would be equal to $100, or times one-hundred, or one hundredfold!!!

And yet hundreds of thousands of Christians would rather have their money in savings accounts at 6-16% interest or in contracts for deed at 10-13%, **while the kingdom of God suffers for lack of finances!!!** We are personally aware of areas of need in the Kingdom of God where souls are going to hell, people are being mobbed, mugged, maimed, mutilated, massacred, or murdered because of men and women, ready to tell the Gospel of the Kingdom are not doing so for lack of finances!! This is so ridic-

ulous, so sad, so frustrating. "Until now the kingdom of God has suffered violence" because men
have not been interested enough, or obedient
enough, or sincere enough, or had faith enough,
or been intense enough, or courageous or loving
enough, or caring enough to take the Kingdom by
force! (Matt. 11:12) But now they are ready and
the finances shall flow.

MAKE A LOAN TO THE LORD

Consider this verse: "He who is gracious to a
poor man lends to the Lord, and He will repay
him for his good deed" Pr. 19:17.

HOW TO SURVIVE DURING THE COMING CRISIS

"Blessed is he that considereth the poor; the
Lord will deliver him in time of trouble" Ps. 41:1
(KJ).

DO YOU BELIEVE THIS VERSE? WILL YOU OBEY IT?

"**Give to him who asks of you,** and **do not
turn away** from him who wants to borrow
from you." (Matt. 5:42). We are asking on behalf
of God's Greater Kingdom. Please understand—I
am as sick as you with the idea of living by "faith
and hints!!!" Or of "faith" broadcasts and ministries who spend most of the time begging for

money (although the beggar Lazarus in Luke 16 went to heaven). We also are deeply aware of verses that declare that "extortioners" or the "covetous" or "swindlers" and "envious" won't inherit the Kingdom of God. This is clear in our minds.

But understand also that there are areas of priority in the Kingdom of God, and there are those who have ministries like those apostles in the New Testament at the feet of whom the first century Christians laid their resources in an administrating or liaison capacity. When we mention resources we do not in any way limit the meaning to money, but also refer to ANY unused talents, abilities, material goods, or any other such potentials to be used in the Kingdom. We have heard the heart's cry of those who have been prepared in the depth of their spirit to be used for the advancement of the Kingdom of God, and we are believing to see these Kingdom resources applied to these Kingdom needs, in order that "this Gospel of the Kingdom shall be preached in all the world for a witness unto all nations; and then shall the end come"!!! Matt. 24:14 (KJ).

VERSES ON KINGDOM RESOURCES

Here are some interesting verses for more information on your resources and God's:

"The generous man will be prosperous, and he who waters will himself be watered." Pr. 11:25

"Give and it will be given to you; good measure, pressed down, shaken together, running over, they will pour into your lap. For whatever measure you deal out to others, it will be dealt to you in return." Luke 6:38

"Sell your possessions and give [alms]: make yourselves purses which do not wear out, an unfailing treasure in heaven, where no thief comes near, nor moth destroys. For where your treasure is, there will be your heart also." Luke 12:33-34

" . . . Remember the words of the Lord Jesus, that He Himself said, 'It is more blessed to give than to receive.' " Acts 20:35

" . . . He who sows sparingly shall also reap sparingly; and he who sows bountifully shall also reap bountifully. Let each one do just as he has purposed in his heart; not grudgingly or under compulsion; for God loves a cheerful giver. And God is able to make all grace abound to you, that always having all sufficiency in everything, you may have an abundance for every good deed." II Cor. 9:6-8

"Now He who supplies seed to the sower and bread for food, will supply and multiply your seed for sowing and increase the harvest of your righteousness; you will be enriched in everything for all liberality which through us is producing thanksgiving to God" II Cor. 9:10-11

We know of families right now who are deeply prepared in the depth of their hearts to serve God, but who are trying to serve God under extreme conditions of financial shortage, while there is more than enough if the people would give. What are you going to tell them? "Be warmed; be blessed; be fed; have faith; if God wills it, it will happen; but I'm going to keep my money!" James 2:14-17 (JB)

I don't believe that the following was the true situation, but for the purposes of illustration, let me share a liberal's interpretation of the feeding of the multitudes by Christ: The story goes that when no one seemed to have any food and everyone seemed hungry, that the little boy willingly gave up his stuff. When the rest of the people saw the boy's unselfishness, they were ashamed and decided to share what they had selfishly been hiding and hoarding; brought their food out and there turned out to be more than enough! (That would really have been a miracle!)

One has described the only difference between heaven and hell as a huge long banquet table on which is set plate fulls of the most fabulous food, but that the people seated have eating instruments attached to their arms in such a way that they are too long to reach their mouths. The hungry first group is so frustrated that they cannot feed themselves, while the people in the second group are feeding each other and having a wonderful time!

While both of the above stories are lacking in

actual fact, the truth exists today that the Gospel of the Kingdom is being terrifyingly hindered through the deep seated selfishness of so many of God's people. But it can also be said that the Kingdom of God is being established as the dear ones are taking courage to give and go and pray and bind and loose for the Kingdom and the Glory of God! Will you join this exciting adventure?!

THE KINGDOM RESOURCES PICTURE

Included is an illustration that should be explained. Kingdom Resources are the resources of the Kingdom of God. They include everything that God has given us, i.e. "every spiritual blessing" (Eph. 1:3), "all things richly to enjoy", (II Tim. 6:17) "all things that pertain to life and godliness" (II Pet. 1:3). These Kingdom Resources include: Salvation, the Lordship of Jesus Christ, the Fullness of God, the Victorious Life, Christ our Life and Righteousness, happy marriages, lives of fruitfulness and fulfillment, fullness of Joy, and the abundant life, etc., and virtually everything we have in God!

By "World Needs" is meant the John 3:16 world God so loves, along with all that they need.

By "Kingdom Need' is meant **all that is needed** to see the Gospel of the Kingdom of God preached in all the world for a witness in all Nations so that the end may come! (Matt. 24:14)

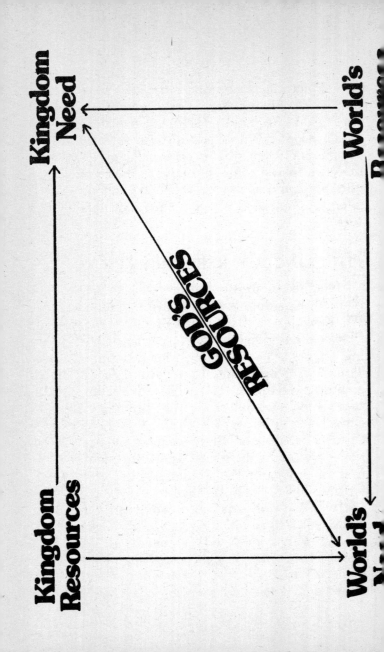

We have discussed that there are terrifying financial needs and need for labourers for the fields
that are white unto harvest! For example, the
country of China is open right now with a billion
people waiting for Bibles and for those to deliver
them. (This can be done for less than $1.00 per
Bible!!) We know of some who are ready to go,
but probably will not go for lack of finances—
unless! If you lined up a billion people shoulder
to shoulder, in a straight line, that line would
reach from here to the moon and half way back,
or at least fourteen times around the world. Will
we fail in this opportunity because the dear ones
will not liquidate their assets in extra boats, cab-
ins, money, clothes, properties, money, investments, savings, junk, possessions, money, securi-
ties, stuff, time, money, energy, prayers, study
time, and money??? The picture is aptly given of
a house on fire with a mother with a baby in her
arms in the upper story of the house with a ladder
lying in the front yard and two people standing
on the sidewalk under the tree having such a
good time they are apparently oblivious to the
terror taking place a few feet away. Paul said,
"Knowing therefore the terror of the Lord, **we
persuade men**!!" We will either have people
pointing their fingers at us from hell saying,
"Why didn't you tell me?" or we will be able to
say with the Apostle, "The blood of no man is on
my hands." O that God could say, "Well done."

By the phrase, "World Resources" is meant

the indescribable wealth and all that is in the earth to complete the fulfillment of the "Great Commission". Recently I read in the newspaper where $110,000 had been left to the care and study of kitty cats in a southern state. The other night, I was looking at a large ad that was begging for money to "save the dogs in Southeast Asia" from being used for food. Seems like some folks are more interested in saving kitty cats than people in the southern U.S. and less interested in helping the starving people in South East Asia than in taking away their dog food. I like doggies and kitties, but the best way to help them is to bring their owners into a walk with God via the Great Commission.

Money is not disappearing. It has just changed hands. There are literally billions and billions and billions of dollars in the hands of the Tri-lateralists, the oil and Opec nations, the international bankers, the insurance companies, the oil companies, etc. There is plenty of money! Also, there are many people that are frustrated because they are at a loss to know what to do with their excess money. Consequently, it ends up not being used for the glory of God. But we must see this money loosed for the telling of the message of God's Kingdom. Consider the following verses:

"Ask of me and I shall give thee the heathen for thine inheritance, and the uttermost parts of the earth for thy possession" Ps. 2:8.

"The wealth of the sinner is laid up for the just" Pr. 13:22.

"You will eat the wealth of Nations, and in their riches you will boast" Isa. 61:6.

"My God shall supply **all** of your needs according to His riches" Ph. 4:19.

"The wealth of the nations will come to you . . . " Isa. 60:5.

"They will bring gold and frankincense . . . " Isa. 60:6.

"Their silver and gold with them . . . " Isa. 60:9.

"And your gates will be open continually; they will not be closed day or night, so that men may bring you the wealth of the nations, with their kings led in procession. For the nation and the kingdom which will not serve you will perish" Isa. 60:11.

But we must tap into the potential of these verses. The time has come for the people of God to wrap themselves with zeal as a cloak, to bind and loose, and to see the theocracy of the King of kings and the Lord of lords established on the earth. **"Thy kingdom come, Thy will be done, on earth as it is in heaven."**

TURN OR BURN

Rev. 11:15:" . . . and the seventh angel sounded; and there were great voices in heaven saying, **"The kingdoms of this world are become the kingdom of our Lord and of His Christ: and He shall reign forever and ever!"** Isaiah 60, just quoted, says, "And the nation and the kingdom which will not serve you shall perish!" (vs. 12)

Let's tell it like it is. If you ain't in the Kingdom of God, you ain't nothin'! It's clearly a case of turn or burn. And baby, **Forever is a long, long time to burn!!!** We choose to serve the Lord willingly in the day of His power. We choose to walk with Him in white. We choose to make God happy! We choose to serve Him gladly. We choose to worship Him freely. How about you? In the name of Yahweh, God of the Universe, **We hereby commission you to be the disciple of the King of Kings and Lord of Lords, the Lord Jesus Christ!!!** In Jesus' Mighty Name, Amen.

Would you read all of Psalm chapter two? Here are the last two verses: "Serve the Lord with fear and rejoice with trembling. Kiss the **Son,** lest He be angry and ye perish from the way." (KJ) "For His wrath may soon [quickly, suddenly, easily] be kindled. How blessed are all who take refuge in Him." (vs. 11, 12)

You will experience the blessing of 10,000% return on everything you invest in the Kingdom of God and have it accredited to your account as having been done to Christ—your worship, your prayers, your life, your time, your money, your love, your possessions, your everything. Amen.

Lord God of the Universe, King of the Nations, we give it all to You. We give You our whole lives, my whole life, now and evermore. Amen.

Review Questions

KINGDOM RESOURCES AND OPPORTUNITIES

1. In banking percentages, what return on your investment is promised in Matt. 19:29, Mark 10:29-30, and Luke 18:28-30?

2. If you invested $1.00 in a bank or finance company, how much would you get back if they promised you a return of a. 1%_____, b. 10%_____, c. 100%_____, d. 1,000%_____, e. 10,000%_____?

3. What return are you presently getting on your investments?

4. What does Matt. 11:12 say?

5. How can we make a loan to the Lord? (Prov. 19:17)

6. How can we survive during the coming crisis? (Ps. 41:1)

7. Are you willing to obey Matt. 5:42 as it pertains to your brother or sister in the Kingdom of God?

8. According to Luke 14:33, how much is it necessary for a disciple to give?

9. Will you be His disciple?

10. Draw the Kingdom Resources diagram.

11. What is perhaps the Greatest single reason why the Great Commission has not been fulfilled?

12. What is the biggest reason why YOU have not been fulfilling the Great Commission (if you have not)?

13. In the "Bibles To China" situation, how many people are in China?

14. How much would it cost, per Bible, for the Chinese people?

15. If you lined up a billion people shoulder to shoulder, how long would the line be? (give two answers)

16. Does the Great Commission apply to you?

17. How specifically do you intend to respond? (Please give some details)

15

GOD WANTS YOUR LOVE!!!
or
KINGDOM WORSHIP

Why? Why was the World created? Why were you created? What does God want the most? What will make Him the happiest?

If we do not know the answer to these questions, we may spend our whole life missing the point in a grand exercise of futility! How will you be clothed in the Kingdom if your total wardrobe is made up of your righteous acts or your living works? Yet, some of us, if we even escape the fire, will escape naked.

But what does the Lord Yahweh want? What can we do to make Him the happiest? The answer to all these questions is simple: Yahweh Sabaoth—God the Lord Jesus Christ—wants our worship. He wants our love to be expressed in praise and adoration.

But one may ask, "What about the righteous acts. Are you becoming works oriented?" We say,

"Of course!" Eph. 2:8-10 and James agree! The Lord Jesus responds, "Let your light so shine before men that they may see your good works and glorify your Father which is in heaven" Matt. 5:16. Also, "By this is My Father glorified, that ye bear MUCH fruit, and so prove to be my disciples" John 15:8. Of course a man is not saved by good works—but to good works!!! Good works are the inevitable result of a love relationship. Our love relationship with Christ.

There seem to be two main hindrances to the Lord God of the Universe receiving adequate praise. One is lack of purity and the second is lack of awareness. The sweet smelling savour of the sacrifice of praise becomes a foul smelling stench in the nostrils of God when there is sin in a person's life. Disunity and barriers in the Body of Christ caused by bitterness, resentment, and lack of fervent love, breaks down and contaminates our communion with the Father. Remember when Christ said that when we bring our gift to the altar and remember that our brother has something against us, we are to leave our gift, go to our brother, make it right, and then come and present our gift (Matt. 5:23-24), I believe this applies to our offerings and tithes, and also to our gifts of praise and songs and service and even the gift of our own life. The Lord El Shaddai must hate discord among the brethren **almost** as much as He hates those that sow that discord among the brethren. (Prov. 6:16-19) No sin. No barriers to love's flow. "Be ye clean that bear the vessels of the Lord" Isa. 52:11 (KJ).

WITHOUT A VISION—
THE PEOPLE PERISH

The second major thing that seems to curtail the praise to the Lord Adonai is our terrifying lack of awareness. "Had they known, they would not have crucified the Lord of Glory." One of the greatest needs is for us to see God's need, God's desire, God's purpose, God's will fulfilled, as the most direct means to seeing our own needs, desires, purposes and will fulfilled. The Word says, "If we keep our life we lose it. If we lose it we gain it" John 12:24-26 (JB). "If we delight ourselves in the Lord, He will give us the desires of our heart!" Ps. 37:4 (JB).

But we have an awful need to know what God wants.

Have you often wondered what it's all about? Why was the world created? What does God want the most? What is the most important thing? What would make God the happiest? What is God's greatest need? What is our greatest need?

To answer these questions with one answer, let us take a look into the heart of God. Jesus says something to us that indicates to us that GOD HAS A NEED. I believe that God has a need!

You may say, "I don't think God needs

anything. God is God. He doesn't need anything from us." But you know, I believe there is one thing that God cannot give to Himself; one thing that God cannot do for Himself; that He needs for us to do for Him; that if we do not do it or be it, that it won't get done or be done. And that is: worship, praise and adoration.

Can you imagine God (or anyone for that matter) looking at Himself in the mirror while making a tape recording of Himself and saying, "You are really wonderful, You are Great, You are powerful, You are precious!?" Can you imagine God trying to praise Himself?

Here is what Jesus said concerning this, "But the hour cometh, and now is, when the true worshippers shall worship the Father in Spirit and in truth; **for the Father seeketh such to worship Him**" John 4:23 (KJ). Again Jesus said, " . . . for it is written, 'Thou shalt worship the Lord thy God, and Him only shalt thou serve' " Matt. 4:10 (KJ)

Can you tune in to the heart of God to see the deep desire that He has for our love and our praise and our worship and our adoration and our thanks??? 'Tis the reason He created us! But how much praise have we given Him today, this week, this year, this life? We have been like frigid wives, or neglectful husbands, unconcerned, self-centered, selfish, and uncaring, or preoccupied with serving Him as a substitute for loving Him. Oh how God loves our praise! Remember the parable of the ten lepers? Of all those healed, only one returned to thank the Lord. This is still another insight into the Heart of God. Remember how angry God became when the ungrateful Israelites gritched and complained even after their marvelous deliverances by the Lord?

HOW MUCH, HOW OFTEN PRAISE?

How much and how often should we praise the Lord?

" . . . let such as love Thy salvation say **continually** , 'Let God be magnified.' " Ps. 70:4b (KJ).

"And my tongue shall speak of Thy righteousness and of Thy praise **all the day long**" Ps. 35:28 (KJ).

"Let them shout for joy, and be glad, that favour my righteous cause: Yea, let them say **continually**, 'Let the Lord be magnified, which hath pleasure in the prosperity of His servant' " Ps. 35:27 (KJ).

"I will bless the Lord **at all times**: His praise shall **continually** be in my mouth" Ps. 34:1 (KJ).

"Giving thanks **always** for all things unto God and the Father in the Name of our Lord Jesus Christ" Eph. 5:20 (KJ).

"Rejoice **evermore**. Pray **without ceasing**. In **every thing** give thanks: for this is the Will of God in Christ Jesus concerning you" I Th. 5:16-18 (KJ).

"Rejoice in the Lord **always**: again I will say rejoice!" Ph. 4:4

HOW SHOULD WE PRAISE GOD?????
100 FOLD RETURN

Here again the promise of the 100 fold return occurs. Some may object at what appears to be an overemphasis on the 10,000% return on our investment in the Kingdom of God, or in God; but please look at this; though we are totally unworthy, God made the provision and gave the promise. When we praise Him, He purposes here again, not to be out given, but to pour us out more than commensurate blessings, more than we shall be able to contain! Alleluyahvah!

HOW SHOULD WE PRAISE GOD?

With all our heart	Ps. 86:12; 111:1; 138:1
Speaking	Ps. 70:4b
Singing	Ps. 21:13; 47:6-7; 7:17; II Chron. 23:13; 29:30; Neh. 12:46
Shouting	Ps. 47:1,5
Dancing	Ps. 149:3
With Instruments	Ps. 150; Harp—33:2; Psaltery—Ps.71:22; Trumpet-Coronet—Ps. 98:6; Cymbal-Tamborine—Ps.149:3, etc.
With upraised hands	Ps. 134:2; 141:2; 143:6;

	28:2; 119:48; I Ki. 8:22; II Chron. 6:13,12; I Tim. 2:8
Uplifted face (prayer)	Mark 6:41; Acts 7:55; II Cor. 3:18; Matt. 14:19
Bowing our heads	Ex. 4:31
Kneeling	II Chron. 6:13
Standing	II Chron. 20:21
On our beds	Ps. 149:5b
With our lives	Gal. 5:25; Phil. 1:21
With the judgments of God	Ps. 76:10
On our faces	Job 1:20; Mt. 2:11; Rev. 11:16; Josh. 5:14; I Cor. 14:25
Greatly	Ps. 48:1
With righteousness	I Ch. 16:29; Ps. 29:2; 96:9
In Spirit	Phil. 3:3; John 4:24
With tongues	I Cor. 12-14
With our understanding	I Cor.12-14
Eating and drinking	I Cor. 10:31
Hymns	Eph. 5:19
Psalms	Eph. 5:19
Spiritual Songs	Eph. 5:19
In truth	John 4:24
With a loud noise	Ps. 98:4

WHERE SHOULD WE PRAISE GOD?

"Among much people" Ps. 35:18

"Unto the ends of the earth" Ps. 48:10

"Among the people— the nations" Ps. 57:9

"In every congregation of the Saints" Ps. 57:9

(In other words—Everywhere)

WHO SHOULD PRAISE GOD?

"Everything that hath breath" Ps. 150:6

"Whoso offereth praise glorifieth Me" Ps. 50:23

"All the people" Ps. 67:3, 5

"Poor and needy" Ps. 74:21

"All nations" Ps. 117:1

"All people" Ps. 117:1

"Everyone" Ps. 148

"Everything" Ps. 148

We recommend the Carothers' books on Praise.

We have a daily contest at our house competing between Karen and the four children and me to see who praises the Lord firstest and mostest. Joshua consistently gets the prize. He's our youngest. He'll say **"HALLELUJAH!"** and I'll say, "Josh gets the prize!" One day he asked me what the prize was. I said, "Josh, the prize is knowing that you make God the happiest by praising Him the firstest and the mostest!" (Tonight at the supper table Josh said "Hallelujah!" right after someone got upset about something. Then someone said, "I'll bet sometimes God gets kinda sick of hearing Josh say 'Howlaylewyuh' ". I said, "I'll bet sometimes God gets kinda sick of **NOT** hearing us say it." Everyone laughed and we all lived happily ever after. What Southern Baptist was it said, "I thank God I praise God more than you all"?

We should praise God how, who, when, where, and why? God wants all of us to praise Him **EVERYWHERE, EVERYONE, ALL THE TIME, EVERY WAY, ALL THE DAY, WITH ALL OUR HEART, SOUL, STRENGTH, MIND AND MIGHT!!!!**

Lord, we repent of being passive and frigid worshipers and determine to excel in the high praises of God!

MINISTERING TO THE KING

We have discovered to our dismay that Christians will do almost anything except wait on God! The flesh and the enemy will accept almost any substitute other than waiting on God. We recommend Andrew Murray's book, "Waiting on

God", a thirty day devotional. Please consider the following verses taken from the King James Version of the Bible:

"Let none that wait on Thee be ashamed . . . " Ps. 25:3a.

" . . . on Thee do I wait all the day" Ps. 25:5c.

"Let integrity and uprightness preserve me; for I wait on Thee" Ps. 25:21.

"Wait on the Lord: be of good courage, and He shall strengthen thine heart: wait, I say, on the Lord" Ps. 37:7.

"Rest in the Lord, and wait patiently for Him . . . " Ps. 37:7.

"For evildoers shall be cut off: but those who wait upon the Lord, they shall inherit the earth" Ps. 37:9.

"Wait on the Lord, and keep His way, and He shall exalt thee to inherit the land: when the wicked are cut off, thou shalt see it" Ps. 37:34.

"And now, Lord, what wait I for? My hope is in Thee" Ps. 39:7.

"I will praise Thee for ever, because Thou hast done it: and I will wait on Thy name; for it is good before Thy saints" Ps. 52:9.

"Because of his [the enemy's] strength will I wait upon Thee: for God is my defence." Ps. 59:9.

"My soul, wait thou only upon God; for my expectation is from Him" Ps. 62:5.

These wait all upon Thee; that Thou mayest give them their meat in due season" Ps. 104:27.

"Behold, as the eyes of servants look unto the

JOHN THE BAPTIST — LEARNING FROM GOD

hand of their masters, and as the eyes of a maiden look unto the hand of her mistress: so our eyes wait upon the Lord our God, until that He have mercy upon us" Ps. 123:2.

"I wait for the Lord, my soul doth wait, and in His word do I hope. My soul waiteth for the Lord more than they that watch for the morning: I say, more than they that watch for the morning" Ps. 130:5-6.

The eyes of all wait upon Thee; and Thou givest them their meat in due season" Ps. 145:15.

All of these scriptures are from the book of Psalms and of course are talking about waiting on God. Here are some other selected scripture references for your benefit if you want some classical verses on waiting on God. We recommend that you take the time to look them up as you wait on God:

Pr. 20:22	Zep. 3:8
Isa. 30:18	Lu. 12:36
Isa. 40:31	Ac. 1:4
Isa. 49:23	Rom. 8:25
Jer. 14:22	Gen. 49:18
Lam. 3:25, 26	Ps. 40:1
Ho. 12:6	Isa. 25:9
Mic. 7:7	Isa. 26:8, 9
Isa. 33:2	Rom. 8:19
Zech. 11:11	Ja. 5:7
Mark 15:43	Pr. 18:34
Ps. 33:20	Lu. 8:40
Ps. 62:1	Rom. 8:23

Ps. 65:1   I Cor. 1:7

Ps. 130:6   II Th. 3:5

Isa. 64:4

Here also are some verses on Seeking the Lord:

De. 4:29	Ps. 24:6
De. 12:5	Ps. 27:4, 8
I Ch. 16:10-11	Ps. 34:10
I Ch. 22:19	Ps. 40:16
I Ch. 28:8, 9	Ps. 53:2
II Ch. 7:14	Ps. 63:1
II Ch. 11:16	Ps. 69:32
II Ch. 12:14	Ps. 70:4
II Ch. 14:4	Ps. 83:16
II Ch. 15:2, 12, 13	Ps. 104:21
II Ch. 19:3	Ps. 105:3, 4
II Ch. 20:3, 4	Ps. 109:10
II Ch. 30:19	Ps. 119:2, 45
II Ch. 31:21	Pr. 8:17
II Ch. 34:3	Pr. 28:5
Ez. 4:2	Isa. 8:19
Ez. 6:21	Isa. 9:13
Ez. 7:10	Isa. 26:9
Ez. 8:21, 22	Isa. 31:1
Ez. 9:12	Isa. 51:1
Job 5:8	Isa. 55:6
Ps. 9:10	Isa. 58:2
Ps. 10:4	Jer. 29:13
Ps. 14:2	Jer. 50:4
Ps. 22:26	Dan. 9:3

Hos. 3:5

Hos. 5:6, 15

Hos. 7:10

Hos. 10:12

Amos 5:4, 6, 8, 14

Amos 8:12

Zep. 2:3

Zec. 8:21, 22

Mal. 3:1

Matt. 6:32, 33

Matt. 7:7

Matt. 28:5

Mark 3:32

Luke 12:29, 30, 31

Luke 13:24

Luke 15:8

Luke 17:33

John 5:30

Acts 15: 17

Acts 17:27

Phil. 2:21

Col. 3:1, 2, 3

Heb. 11:6

Why is it that people will go to meetings, but will not seek the Lord? Or read His Word? Why will people go to Bible School, seminary, and Bible College, but will not wait on God? Why do so many pastors, evangelists, apostles, teachers and even missionaries not wait on God? They will go to movies, meetings, picnics, schools, churches, mission fields, but not wait on God!

I suppose one reason we haven't waited on or sought God more is our "work ethic syndrome". Our thinking has been that if we are not "doing" something, then we are not being "productive". We have considered waiting on God, fasting, seeking God, prayer, intercession, travail, being silent before the Lord as **"down time"**!!!, or unproductive or unfruitful or wasted time.

Oh, may God help us to see that without seeking God and waiting on God, our lives become wasted time, energy, talent, words and effort. **Our life becomes a grand exercise in futility in direct proportion to our lack of time spent before the Lord.** "But without faith it is impossible to please Him: for he that cometh to God must believe that He is, and that **He is a rewarder of them that diligently seek Him**" Heb. 11:6.

Again, please remember the correlation between our relationship with God and that of many who have a spouse who is so busy **doing for them,** that they have little or no time to spend **with them.**

If we are too busy to wait on God, then **we are too busy!!!!!!!**

But now comes a new revelation to us of the importance of our waiting on God. Now comes a full release to our hearts to spend precious time before God's Presence.

HOW TO WAIT ON GOD

Rule number ONE: ......W—A—I—T—!!!!
Rule number TWO: ......W—A—I—T—!!!!
Rule number THREE: ...W—A—I—T—!!!!

We suggest that at all costs, you immediately make plans to be able to spend precious time with the Lord. Alone. Quietly. Without distractions. Make it a way of life. Give up something of lesser importance in order to have some precious time with the Lord. There is **no substitute for waiting on God!!!!**

This time must be spent in quiet listening for the Lord, looking for Him, waiting for Him, listening to Him, concentrating on Him. This time must be in addition to singing, praying out loud, voicing your requests, reading a good book, reading the Bible or sleeping. This exercise must become a way of life for us.

Now is the time for earnest, deep and sweet repentance of the kind that causes us to change our life in this matter.

An apostle friend said that God spoke that He is grieved that His people do not seek Him or wait on Him enough to become that perfected Bride He is seeking. My friend asked God how this problem would be solved. God spoke that He would allow affliction and adversity to come. Then His people would seek Him. (Ps. 119:67, 71; 78:34; 77:2). But listen my friends, let's be determined to seek God without needing the incentive of affliction!

Lord Jesus Christ, Father God, we repent of our spiritual frigidity and the luke warm leaving of our first fervent love for Thee. Oh, the delight of spending precious time and times with Thee! Oh, the transport of being in Thy presence! Oh, the rapture all divine! Oh, the wonder of Thy Glory! Oh, the Beauty of Thy Love! Thank You, Thank You, Thank You, Lord God of Hosts!!!!

Review Questions

WHAT IT'S ALL ABOUT!

1. Why were you created?
2. What does God want the most?
3. Give some reasons why we don't praise the Lord more.
4. What is one thing God cannot or will not do for Himself or give Himself?
5. Who should praise the Lord?
6. When should we praise the Lord?
7. How should we praise the Lord?
8. Where should we praise the Lord?
9. Why should we praise the Lord?
10. In our walk with God, what is it almost easier to do anything but?

16

HOW CAN WE RULE
THE WORLD?
or
KINGDOM GLORY

Outline

Rev. 2:26-28, "We can rule over the nations with a rod of iron." (JB)

Matt. 5:5, "We can inherit the earth." (JB)

I Cor. 6:3, "We shall judge angels."

Daniel 7:18, 22, 27, "The time arrived when the saints **took** possession of the Kingdom."

Ps. 2:6-9, "People and land as our possession." (JB)

Ps. 149:4-9, We can "bind the kings with chains."

Joel 2:1-11, We, The Invincible.

Ps. 16:3, "But to the Saints that are in the earth, and to the excellent in whom is all My delight." (KJ)

John 10:34-35, "Jesus said, 'Ye are gods!' "

Rev. 12:13, Caught up to a place of authority.

Rev. 19:14, Riding with Him on our big white horses.

I John 2:6, We can walk just like He did.

I John 4:17, We can be like Christ now.

II Cor. 2:14, Victory, always, everyplace.

Rev. 1:12-17, Our face can shine like the sun.

Rev. 19:10, John worshipped his brother?

Rev. 22:8, He worshipped a prophet?

Matt. 18:18, "Whatsoever ye bind . . ."

Ph. 4:13, Our omnipotence.

John 14:12, Greater works than Christ.

Galatians 2:20, Christ my life.

HOW CAN WE RULE THE WORLD?

Here we have several easy lessons on "How to rule the world!" My little boy, Joshua, asked me the other day, "Dad, when we get to heaven, are we going to be angels?" And before I could think of how to answer, Josh answered his own question by saying, "Oh, I know! We won't be angels because we are going to be judging and ruling over the angels!" I thought of that scripture, I Cor. 6:3: "Do you not know that we shall judge angels? How much more matters of this life?" Pretty good for a little boy, eh? But notice also verse 2, Or "do you not know that the saints will **judge the world**?"

I would like to let you in on a little big secret. **God is looking for persons to whom He**

wants to give His unlimited power, and authority, and love, and joy, and financial provision and miracle power, but God will not give these things to people who are not prepared or who have not been faithful! He will not give unlimited power to someone who will prostitute it or do his own thing with it. **God is looking for those who are holy, are overcomers, are willing to do anything God says, who have learned His voice, and are totally sold out to Jesus Christ as Lord. Amen!**

There is a special kind of people the Lord talks about, special not because of anything good about their old nature (except that it's dead). But God's invitation is open to everyone! "Whosoever will, may come" and the Bible says, "God is no respecter of persons, [does not show partiality]" Acts 10:34 (KJ). Nevertheless, only those among us that are overcomers and holy ones will qualify! (those who are not man pleasers, but who **do** the will of God.)

The following phrases are used to describe these people who will rule the world. Then I will tell you how you can be one of them!

"**As for the saints** (lit., Holy Ones; i.e., the Godly) who are in the earth, they are the **MAJESTIC ONES** (the **excellent** KJ) in whom is **all** My delight" Ps. 16:3. ("The Majestic Ones", sounds like a good movie or book title, eh?!)

"For the **Lord** [YAHWEH] takes pleasure

in **His people**. He will beautify **the afflicted ones** with salvation. Let The **Godly ones** exult in glory; Let **them** sing for joy on their beds. Let the high praises of God be in their mouth, and a two-edged sword in their hand, to execute vengeance on the nations, and punishment on the peoples; to bind their kings with chains, and their nobles with fetters of iron; to execute on them the judgment written; this is an honor for **all His godly ones**." Ps. 149:4-9. **Allelujahvah!!!!**

The whole of Psalm two talks about the same thing, especially verses 6-9:

"But as for me I have installed My King upon Zion, My holy mountain. I will surely tell of the decree of the Lord: He said to **me**, Thou are My Son, today I have begotten Thee. Ask of Me, and I will surely give the nations as Thy inheritance, and the very ends of the earth as Thy possession. Thou shalt break them with a rod of iron, Thou shalt shatter them like earthenware.' "

The first half of Joel chapter two talks about the same thing, especially verses 1-11. (Read aloud with super gusto)

"Blow a trumpet in Zion, and sound an alarm on My holy mountain! Let all the inhabitants of the land tremble, For the day of the Lord is coming; Surely it is near, A day of darkness and gloom, A day of clouds and thick darkness. As the dawn is spread over the mountains, So there is a great and mighty people; There has never been anything like it, Nor will there be again after it to the years of many generations. A fire consumes before them, and behind them, a flame burns. The land is like the garden of Eden before them, But a desolate wilderness behind them, and nothing at all escapes them. Their appearance is like the appearance of horses; and like war horses, so they run. With a noise as of chariots they leap on the tops of the mountains, like the crackling of a flame of fire consuming the stubble, like a mighty people arranged for battle. Before them the peoples are in anguish; all faces turn pale. They run like mighty men; They climb the wall like soldiers; and they march each in line, nor do they deviate from their paths. They do not crowd each other; they march every one in his path. When they burst through the defenses, they do not break ranks. They rush on the city, they run on the wall; they climb into the houses, they enter through the windows like a thief. Before them the earth quakes, the heavens tremble, the sun and the moon grow dark, and the stars lose their brightness. And the Lord utters His voice before His army; surely His camp is very great, for **strong is He who carries out His Word**. The day of the Lord is indeed great and very awesome, and who can endure it?" Joel 2:1-11.

I believe if you carry out His word, can endure His day, and can grasp the ideas presented here, you can quote the above paragraph in the 1st person!!! Now read it again. Can you visualize yourself as one of the invincible ones?

The Book of Revelation chapter two talks about the same thing:

> "And **he who overcomes,** and **he who keeps My deeds** until the end, to him **I will** give **authority over the nations;** and he shall rule them with a rod of iron, as the vessels of the potter are broken to pieces, as I also have received authority from My Father and I will give him the morning star." Rev. 2:26-28

Daniel talks much about the Kingdom of God. Here is a sample:

> "Until the Ancient of Days came, and judgment was passed in favor of **the holy ones (the saints)** of the Highest One, and the **time arrived** when the **saints** took possession of the Kingdom." Dan. 7:22

> "Then the Kingdom, (sovereignty), the dominion, and the Greatness of all the kingdoms under the whole heaven will be given to the **people of the holy ones,** (saints) of the Highest One; His Kingdom will be an Everlasting Kingdom, and all the dominions will serve and obey Him." Dan. 7:27

Perhaps you have been wondering how to become one of these people. Perhaps you, too, would like to rule the world. Here's how:

1. Receive Christ as your Saviour, Lord and Life.
2. Be aware, on a revelation level, that you are seated in Christ in the heavens. Eph. 1

& 2 and Col. 3 tells us this fact: that not only did Christ take us with Him to the cross and the tomb, but also with Him to the very heavens in the throne room of the Father and caused us to Be seated **in** Christ Jesus, far over and above every principality and power, and over everything that is named in heaven or on earth!!" (JB) Here we are with Him now, and we "have the mind of Christ". (I Cor. 2:16)

With everything that we have in God, **two things are necessary. First,** we need a revelation of the provision, not just "head knowledge." **Second**, we need to act on the basis of the accomplished fact of healing, and miracle power, Christ as our life, or as **our** Righteousness, and that He has taken us to be **seated in Christ our life**. In each case we need a revelation of it so that we know that **we know** that **we know!** The only other thing that's necessary for anything we potentially have in God, is to **act on the basis of the accomplished fact!** *Faith always acts on what it believes.* Faith without corresponding action is dead!

For example, a person could be starving to death even though he may have closet shelves lined with food, if he doesn't **know the provision is there** or if he doesn't **act on the basis of the provision.** A person could have a million dollars in his bank account but not be able to buy a thing if he is not **aware of the provision**, or if he does not write a check and **live on the basis of the accomplished fact**!

The story is told of Ole and Sven coming over on the boat to the new country from the old country. Ole only had enough money for his ticket but only pennies extra for food. So, he thought, "Hmm, let's see now, what's the most amount of food I can buy for the least amount of money for the boat ride?" So he finally decided to buy a sack of potatoes which he took to his room. All the way across, he ate potatoes, raw, one each meal. When they were pulling into New York, past the Statue of Liberty, Sven saw Ole at the rail all hungry looking and said to him, "Why, Ole, how come I never seen you in the dining room on this trip?" And upon hearing about the bag of potatoes, one each meal, Sven said, "Why didn't ye know that all of those ship's huge and lavish banquet meals vas included in the price of the ticket?!."

Another story is told of a man who died and went to heaven to be shown around by Saint Peter, who took him to a huge warehouse in which were endless shelves loaded with beautifully wrapped presents. The person asked Peter what the presents were, whereupon Peter explained, "These are all the lovely things the Heavenly Father intended for you to have on earth, but because you didn't open and enjoy them then, you may have them now! !"

I really don't think that the above two stories are very scriptural though, because of Christ's parable of the "One talent" man. When he failed to appropriate his possessions and multiply his talent, what he did have was taken away, given to another, while he was exiled to the blackness of outer darkness, with wailing and gnashing of teeth and given an eternal existence. (Matt. 25:30)

I don't really see that we have much of an option, dear one. It's either be **overcome** or an **overcomer!** A man of God said, "Show me a good loser, and I'll show you a loser." I'm not sure who he was quoting, but if one doesn't, overcome, he is surely not an overcomer. I can't get over some theologians saying that a sinner is a saint, and that God is blind or wears rose colored glasses and can't see our sin because we're hiding behind Christ. That's garbage. The Father, Son and Holy Spirit and the great cloud of witnesses see us as we are.

The Bible says, "Follow . . . holiness, without which no man shall see the Lord" and believe God, dear theologian, it's talking about gut-level-git-down-where-we-live practical holiness. That's the only kind there is anyway. Or are you one of those protestants that believes in purgatory? You ask them, "Are you holy now?" They say, "Oh, no we can't be pure, righteous, holy or perfect this side of the grave!" You ask them,

"Do you believe the Word, 'without holiness, no man shall see the Lord' ?" (Heb. 12:14) They say, with a kind of dumb expression on their face, "Well some time between the time I die and the time I get to heaven, God's gonna do an abra-ka-dabra on me and make me perfect" (instantaneous purgatory)!!

O.K. Folks, let's all wipe the dumb look off our faces and come out into the Light Of His Shining Glory, confess our sins, and be cleansed from ALL unrighteousness not "some" or "most" but all!!! Today—Now!

THE GLORY—OURS

There is something here that you may not be ready for in your thinking unless you really, REALLY, want to walk with Him. The Lord Jesus Christ who has come in the flesh, has come in our flesh, and will come in the clouds when every eye shall see Him. And that is this thing of the KINGDOM GLORY. Here are some examples:

In Exodus 34:29-35, the account is given where Moses had been in the presence of the Lord God of the Universe, and his face shone so that the Israelites could not stand to look upon his face, so that he had to put a veil over his face in order to talk to the people. Apostle Paul, talking about this, repeats himself being almost loquatiously, verbosely redundant. Four times he makes the point that this Glory of Moses was **nothing by comparison** to the **glory that is available to us right now!** He concludes II Cor. 3:18 by saying that, "We **all . . . beholding . . . the glory of the Lord are changed into the same image**". (KJ) And in chapter 4 he said, "**For God who said, 'light shall shine out of darkness' is the One who has shone in our hearts to give the light of the knowledge of the glory of God in the face of Christ.**" (vs. 6)

Did you know that you can have an experience with Christ **more real** than if you fell dead and Jesus was looking for a body through whom He wanted to **live in the earth?** Let's pretend that Christ came into your warm but dead body and became your life, speaking His Words through your lips, blessing through your hands, loving people through you, but incognito, or in disguise in you. There is something better than this; and that is appropriating Christ to be our life by faith. And the Christ that becomes our life is not the unglorified Christ but the Glorified One. God says that we can walk as Christ walked (I John 2:6) and that we can be **as Christ is**, in this **present world**!!! I John 4:17.

Please look with me in Revelation 19 where John the Beloved Apostle does something seemingly cultic. Verse 10 says, "And I (John) fell at his feet to worship him. And he said to me, 'Do not do that; I am a fellow-servant of yours and your brethren who hold the testimony of Jesus;

worship God." What on earth prompted John to do such a thing as that!? Surely he knew better! He walked with Christ on earth for three years, leaned his head on Jesus, and was perhaps the closest to Christ. And John saw what Christ looked like in His Glorified state in Revelation chapter 1. So please tell me, dear one, **why did John fall down and worship this brother in the Lord?** The brother in the Lord said, "I'm just your brother, just a fellow-servant. Don't worship me, worship God!" Well anyway, it looks like John has learned his lesson.

But let's look at Revelation chapter 22 where John "messes up" again! He does something borderline cultic. "And I, John, am the one who heard and saw these things. And when I heard and saw, I fell down to worship at the feet of the [messenger] who showed me these things. And he said to me, 'Do not do that; I am a **fellow servant** of yours and of your **brethren the prophets, and of those who keep the words of this book! Worship God!**' " (vs. 8-0)

HE COULDN'T TELL THE DIFFERENCE!

I believe the reason why John fell down to worship at the feet of his brother in the Lord was that **he could not tell the difference**!!! I believe that this fellow servant-brother-prophet had gotten hold of this secret we are presenting, and that he was walking **"As Christ Walked"**! I believe this disciple messenger had gotten hold of the truth that, **"As Christ is so are we in this present world!"**

I may be mistaken, but I believe that the brother that was talking to John looked like this:

His eyes shown like a flame of fire!

His face shone like the sun in its strength!

His feet glowed as bronze heated to white hot intensity!

His voice was as the sound of many waters!

Dear one, if you forget all else in this book, always remember that Christ has called you and me to be **"As Christ is . . . in this present world!!"** I believe we are to be so much like Christ that like Paul and Barnabas we will need the integrity to explain to people that there is a difference. (Acts 14) There must be no limitation that we place on the Lord's desire and ability to manifest His life and glory through us, though the glory must always belong to Him. Amen!!!

KINGDOM POWER

"For the Kingdom of God does not consist in words, but in Power." I Cor. 4:20.

"Thy right hand, O LORD, is become majestic [glorious] in Power: Thy right hand, **O Lord,** shatters [hath dashed in pieces] the enemy" Ex. 15:6.

"Thine, **O Lord,** is the greatness, and the

Power, and the glory, and the victory and the majesty: for all that is in the heaven and in the earth is Thine; Thine is the Kingdom, **O Lord**, and Thou art exalted as head above all; and in Thine hand is power and might; and in Thine hand it is to make great, and to give strength unto all. Now therefore, our God, we thank Thee, and praise Thy glorious name" I Chron. 29:11-13 ((KJ).

"He ruleth by His power for ever; His eyes behold the nations: let now the rebellious exalt themselves" Ps. 66:7 (KJ).

"Sing unto God, ye kingdoms of the earth; O sing praises unto the Lord; to Him that rideth upon the heavens of heavens, which were of old; lo, He doth send out His voice, and that a mighty voice. Ascribe ye strength unto God; His excellency is over Israel, and His strength is in the clouds. O God, Thou art terrible out of Thy holy places: the God of Israel is He that giveth strength and power unto his people. Blessed be God" Ps. 68:32-35 (KJ).

"All Thy works shall praise Thee, **O Lord**; and Thy saints shall bless Thee. They shall speak of the glory of Thy Kingdom and talk of Thy power; to make known to the sons of men His mighty acts, and the glorious majesty of His Kingdom. Thy Kingdom is an everlasting Kingdom, and Thy dominion endureth throughout all generations" Ps. 145:10-13 (KJ).

" . . . for Thine is the Kingdom and the power and the glory forever. Amen" Matt. 6:13 (KJ).

" . . . He gave them power (authority) over unclean spirits, to cast them out and to heal every kind of disease and every kind of sickness" Matt. 10:1 (KJ).

"And Jesus came and spake unto them, saying, "All power is given unto Me in heaven and in earth." Matt. 28:18b

" . . . He (Jesus) gave them power and authority over all demons, and to heal diseases, and He sent them out to proclaim the Kingdom of God, and perform healing" Luke 9:1, 2.

"Until you are clothed with power from on high" Luke 24:49.

"But you shall receive power when the Holy Spirit is come upon you, and you shall be My witnesses . . . even to the remotest parts of the earth." Acts 1:8

"And Steven, full of grace and power, was performing great wonders and signs among the people." Acts 6:8

"Now may the God of hope fill you with all joy and peace in believing, that you may abound in hope by the power of the Holy Spirit." Rom. 15:13

"In the power of signs and wonders, in the power of the Spirit, so that . . . I have fully preached the gospel of Christ" Rom. 15:19.

"And my message and my preaching were not in persuasive words of wisdom, but in demonstration of the Spirit and of power. That your faith should not rest on the wisdom of men, but on the power of God" I Cor. 2:4, 5.

"For the Kingdom of God does not consist in words, but in power" I Cor. 4:20.

"But we have this treasure in earthen vessels, that the greatness of [His] power may be of God and not from ourselves" II Cor. 4:7.

"For our gospel did not come to you in word only, but also in power and in the Holy Spirit and with full conviction" I Th. 1:5.

"For God has not given us a spirit of [fear], but of power and love and of sound judgment. Therefore do not be ashamed of the testimony of our Lord, or of me His prisoner; but join with me suffering for the Gospel according to the power of God" II Tim. 1:7-8.

"Holding to a form of godliness although they have denied its power and avoid such men as these" II Tim. 3:5.

"Seeing that His divine power has granted to us everything pertaining to life and godliness, through the true knowledge of Him who has called us by His own glory and excellence" II Pet. 1:3.

"For we did not follow cleverly devised tales, when we made known unto you the power and coming of our Lord Jesus Christ, but were eye-witnesses of His majesty" II Pet. 1:16.

"Finally brethren, be strong in the Lord and in the [power] of His might" Eph. 6:10.

"And he who overcomes and he who keeps My deeds until the end, to him I will give [power] authority over the Nations. And he shall rule them with a rod of iron as the vessels of the potter are broken to pieces, as I also have received authority from My Father" Rev. 2:26-27.

KINGDOM AUTHORITY

What words did Joshua use in the performing of the miracle of the sun standing still? No plaintive pleading, he said, "Sun, stand thou still, and moon refuse to rise" Joshua 10:12 (JB). It is interesting that Exodus 14:15 says, "Then the Lord said to Moses, 'Why are you crying out to Me? Tell the sons of Israel to go forward." There is no evidence that David prayed when he went after Goliath, but he prophesied his death, "This day will the Lord deliver you up into my hands, and I will strike you down and remove your head from you." (I Sam. 17:46) Nor is there any evidence that Jonathan and the armorbearer prayed when they went and made it happen. It was like they flipped a coin as a type of fleece, to determine the plan of action. It was as if they said, "Heads, we gonna go make it happen, or tails we gonna go make it happen" (I Sam. 14:9-10 JB). Another thing that is interesting is that with the exception of the Red Sea, there is no evidence that God specifically **told** them to do what they did. In each case, there was something that needed to be done . . . and they did it. When Jesus did His miracles, He almost never prayed publicly, He just spoke it into existence. For example, Jesus said to the storm, "Peace, be still," (Mark 4:39) Or to the little dead girl, "Maid, I say unto thee, arise," (Mk. 5:41) Or to Lazarus, "Lazarus, come forth." (John 11:43) Or to the deaf man, "Be opened." (Mark 7:34) Or to the fig tree, "Be cursed." (Mark 11:14 JB)

At the gate Beautiful, the apostles didn't pray. They just said, "Such as we have [the Name of Jesus] give we unto you. Rise up and walk" Acts 3:6. We are not against praying— except when we use it as an excuse for disobedience.

Do you see the point we are trying to make? We will increase our doing of the will of God when we stop leaving the responsibility for God to do what He has given us the responsibility to do! We already talked about that. But here's how we do it. We **speak it into existence with a word of faith and authority**!!!, coupled with accompanying actions that give expression to our faith. Too often we've done a plaintive pleading to the Lord when He wants us to **make it happen**. "What you bind will be bound", Jesus says. "If two of you agree it shall be done. If you loose, it will be loosed" Matt. 18:18.

I was noticing in Genesis 1 the way the worlds were created. God would say, "Let there be . . . " and there was! Then God would call something "Good" and it was!!!

Hebrews comments about this in 11:3,

"Through faith we understand that the worlds (or ages) were framed by the Word of God, so that the things which are seen were not made of things which do appear." **That's how we do the will of God today!! We speak things into existence by the word of faith coupled with appropriate faith action!!!!** And that's how all those "good ol' boys" did the works of God! That is how we will do the works of God. A number of years ago, I became frustrated with God because He didn't raise someone up that we were asking God to heal. In my frustration I said to God, "When I get to heaven, Lord, I'm going to ask You why You didn't heal this lady", and it seemed like the Lord answered right back by saying, "And when you ask Me, John, I am going to ask you why **you** didn't heal her!"

The Lord is still saying to us, **"Wherefore criest thou unto Me? Speak it into existence!!"** Please understand, we aren't against prayer. In fact, "We ought always to pray, and not to faint" Luke 18:1. But there's a time for prayer and there's a time for "making it happen" in Christ!

God told Joshua, after Ai, "Get up off your face, there's sin in the camp!" Joshua 7:10 (JB). And God told Samuel who prayed and cried all night for Saul, "Stop crying, and go anoint someone else" I Sam. 16:1 (JB). We are against the prayer of plaintive whining as a substitute for getting the job done. Faith without works is dead, James 2:17. And so are we if we are "hearers of the word only" James 1:22. And so is the Great Commission without its accompanying obedience! Please pray with me.

Lord God of Sovereign Action—Act sovereignly in us, through us, in Your miraculous creative way again. Thank You, Mighty Right Now God, for working in us both to will and to **do** of Your good pleasure! We repent of waiting for You to do what You've been waiting for us to do while all the while the weapons of our warfare have been mighty through God to the tearing down of strongholds. Be all that You are in us. Cause us to be those people of the Shining and Radiant countenance. We volunteer to be the Joel's army of God, and will pay whatever price is necessary to walk with You in white—and rule the world with You on Your throne!!!

Review Questions

HOW CAN WE RULE THE WORLD?

1. Will we be angels in heaven?
2. Will God give His unlimited power, glory and wealth to unprepared or undependable people?
3. List at least 4 synonyms or similar phrases that describe who the "overcomers" are.
4. Name the 5 things that the saints are privileged to do in Psalm 149:7-9.
5. Who is Joel's Army in Joel 2:1-11?
6. What three things are given the overcomers in Rev. 2:26-28?
7. Who took possession of the Kingdom in Daniel 7:22? _____ In Matthew 11:12? _____ In each case, who are these talking about?
8. What 2 things are always necessary in order for us to walk in the provision of the Lord?
9. Do you think the one talent man in Matthew 25:30 had been born again?
10. What happened to the one talent man?
11. Are you a saint or holy? Do you expect to be? When?
12. Do you think it is possible to walk as Christ walked?
13. Describe at least four things about Christ's appearance in Revelation chapter one.

14. Is it possible to be as Christ is in this world?

15. Why did John fall down to worship at the feet of his brother in Rev. 19:10 and 22:9?

16. In those passages, what did John's brother do or say that we should also do or say when people try to worship us?

17. Do you think we should live in such a way that people would try to or want to worship us?

18. Please try to quote or refer to at least three verses in the Bible that talk about the power of God.

19. By what method did God create the world?

20. Give at least three scriptural examples in the Bible where men of God, including Jesus, spoke directly to inanimate objects or things by way of creative command.

21. Give at least one scriptural example where God told someone to stop praying.

17

GOD'S VISION . . .
WE HAVE A VISION
I HAVE A VISION
PLEASE, HAVE GOD'S VISION

God's vision is to see the Gospel of the Kingdom preached to the uttermost part of the world. The desire of our hearts for this book is to open opportunities to present the Good News of the Kingdom of God to those who would present the Good News of the Kingdom of God!!!, in the fulfillment of the Great Commission.

Would you seek God? Would you seek God very earnestly? Would you seek God from your heart to see whether or not you will share the vision of the Great Commission? Would you seek God deep in your heart to make God's vision **your vision?**

As we have stated before, our whole desire is to do God's will. If we can be of any help, in any way that will promote the Kingdom of God on earth, please call on us. Our present address and phone number are on the back cover of this book. We thank God for the response to His Divine Call to the Dynamic Destiny of Discipleship!

There are available to you representatives of the Kingdom of God to come to your area for classes, seminars, sermons, on more than the following areas, including the material taught in this book: Marriage and family, Discipleship training, the Lordship of Christ, the Fullness of God, Church Growth and Renewal, and the **Kingdom of God.**

. . . THE GREAT COMMISSION

Now hear the God of all Heaven and Earth speak to you now, a crystal clear, sure and pure, "thus saith the Lord," . . . **"SEEK YE FIRST THE KINGDOM OF GOD, AND HIS RIGHTEOUSNESS; AND ALL THESE THINGS WILL BE ADDED UNTO YOU!!!"**

GO YE THEREFORE AND TEACH [MAKE DISCIPLES OF] ALL NATIONS, BAPTIZING THEM IN THE NAME OF THE FATHER, AND OF THE SON, AND OF THE HOLY GHOST.

TEACHING THEM TO OBEY ALL THINGS WHATSOEVER I HAVE COMMANDED YOU. AND LO, I AM WITH YOU ALWAYS, EVEN UNTO THE END OF THE WORLD. AMEN.

KINGDOM QUESTIONS
(Please Respond)

1. Do you know of anyone that could benefit from any part of the Kingdom of God in terms of counselling, prayer, training, personal ministry, visitation, encouragement, seminars or additional copies of this book, etc.?

2. Do you know of any source that has abilities or resources they would like to volunteer for the cause of the advancement of the Gospel of the Kingdom?

3. Do you personally have any needs the Kingdom of God could meet such as prayer, encouragement, counselling, fellowship, books, seminars, commissioning, training, etc.?

4. Do you personally have any gifts or abilities, time or talents, money or possessions that you would be willing to volunteer to the cause of Christ as it relates to the Kingdom of God and to the spreading of the Gospel of the Kingdom? On a short term basis; or long term; or monthly basis?

5. Do you know of any group or church that could benefit in any way from the resources of the Kingdom of God in terms of retreats, conferences, meetings, seminars, teaching, Bible studies, speakers, etc.?, on the subjects of Discipleship-Leadership Training, Church Growth and Renewal, Marriage and Family,

etc.?

6. Do you have any constructive counsel for this presentation? Other ideas for the outreach of the Gospel of the Kingdom? Anything to offer that would be of help?

7. Would you be interested in fellowship or getting to know others that also have an unreserved discipleship commitment to Jesus Christ the Lord and King?

8. Are you willing to give and live your life completely to the King of kings, and Lord of lords, to seek first the Kingdom of God and His righteousness?

9. Has this book been a blessing to you? We would like to know.

10. Would you be interested in contributing or helping to get this book into the hands of those not able to pay for it, i.e., the poor, "shut-in's," prisoners, other countries, students, hospitalized, etc.?

11. Do you know of anyone who would like this book on tape or in another language?

12. Would you like a copy or copies of the Kingdom Contract evangelism brochure?

13. Would you like to have additional copies of this book? It was designed for use in any of the following ways: Seminary, Bible College, Bible School, Sunday School, Seminars, Conferences, Church Renewal, Discipleship-Leadership Training, Personal Study, Family Devotions, Home Meetings, Classroom

Curriculum, Men's, Women's, or Children's Meetings, Sermon or Teaching Series, publication in periodicals, etc.

14. Would you like to be kept informed of new books or developments relating to the ministry of the Great Commission?

All correspondence may be directed to:
        The Kingdom of God
        % John Bohlen, a representative
        P.O. Box 7123
        Minneapolis, Minnesota 55407

This book is also available on tape cassettes.

(All gifts to The Kingdom of God are tax deductible)

OPPORTUNITY!

You can help fulfill the Great Commission through book sales and distribution, along with other Christian Bibles, books, tapes and records, while at the same time obtaining your own material at a discount or for profit to you and your organization.

This book, for example, could be ordered as follows:

Single copy	@ $4.95 each
5 to 10 copies	@ $4.50 each
10 to 20 copies	@ $3.95 each
20 to 50 copies	@ $3.50 each
50 to 100 copies	@ $2.95 each
100 or more copies	@ $2.50 each
One Album of 6 cassettes	@ $34.95 each
2 to 5 Albums of 6 cassettes	@ $29.95 each
5 to 10 Albums of 6 cassettes	@ $24.95 each
10 to 20 Albums of 6 cassettes	@ $19.95 each
20 or more	@ $14.95 each

Similar arrangements can be made on other Bibles, books, tapes, records, etc. You may send inquiries to:

The Kingdom of God
Box 7123
Minneapolis, Minnesota 55407

or call area code 612-823-1783. All profits from this book, or contributions, are used for the fulfillment of the Great Commission.